BURN

LIVE THE COMPASSION OF JESUS

(**BRIAN SHIPMAN**)

THOMAS NELSON PUBLISHERS®
Nashville

A Division of Thomas Nelson, Inc.

To Ryan, my firstborn,
Whose little heart
Has made mine so much bigger

. . .

The publisher thanks The Livingstone Corporation for their assistance with this title.

Published in Nashville, Tennessee, by Thomas Nelson, Inc.

Scripture quotations are from THE NEW KING JAMES VERSION. Copyright © 1979, 1980, 1982, Thomas Nelson, Inc., Publishers.

ISBN 0-7852-6746-8

Printed in the United States of America.

CONTENTS

Preface   iv

1. What Is Compassion?   1

2. People You Don't Know   8

3. People in Your Family   19

4. People Who Lead You   32

5. People Who Serve You   47

6. People Who Don't Know Jesus   59

7. People You Call Friends   76

8. People You Call Enemies   91

9. People Who Need Forgiveness   108

10. People Who Are Sick   124

11. People in Your Church   141

12. People Who Need Encouragement   158

13. People Who Are Different   175

    Ministry Opportunities   187

    Other Xt4J Products   188

PREFACE

This book is set up as a simple, three-step plan. Its purpose is to help you make the connections from Jesus' life to yours. So, as you read each chapter, make sure you have your Bible alongside it. (#1) Let God's amazing Word penetrate your soul and change you. (#2) Blow past the roadblocks—or excuses—keeping you from living compassionately. (#3) Burn it home—go *do* what you read. Get out there and burn some compassion into someone else's mind. Make a lasting impression.

I want to thank a group of people for helping me bring this book to life. To Jesus, thank you for giving me this opportunity and for never giving up on me.

To my incredible bride, Jennifer, for being a constant reminder of what it means to be compassionate.

To my friend, Mike, for walking with me and shoving me onward and upward during the tough times.

To my good friends Derrick, Kara, Scott, Robin, Ron, Ann, Jeff, and Leann at Pantego Bible Church, for praying me through the final weeks of this project.

Now get going. The fire has already started, and God is looking for a few good hearts that are ready to burn for him. Will yours be one?

It was Melissa's eighteenth birthday. She planned to celebrate big time later on, but for now she was rotting away in line. Her driver's license expired today, and so she stood bored to tears in the Department of Motor Vehicles—always a fun place to spend your birthday. She passed the time by daydreaming and people watching. The musty little room was quiet, and each stranger stared glassy-eyed at the floor or at all the government notices posted on one side of the room. After what seemed like forever (really only an hour), she finally arrived at the front of the line. At last!

The door to the DMV opened. Melissa noticed a frail, little older woman with a cane walk inside. The woman looked shocked when she saw the length of the line (now even longer than when Melissa came). She sighed and quietly took her place at the back. Melissa realized that the woman would be on her feet for at least an hour. She looked at her own place in line and then back at the elderly woman's. She couldn't help wondering,

What would Jesus do now? *The answer was so clear, it hit her with a jolt.*

"Ma'am," Melissa said, motioning to the woman in the back and breaking the silence, her voice echoing along the tile floor. "Why don't you come up here and take my place in line?" The stunned woman stared at Melissa, not sure whether she was joking. Melissa asked the man behind her to hold her place. While everyone else watched in shock, she escorted the woman to the front of the line. Just as they arrived, the clerk shouted, "Next!"

The elderly woman squeezed Melissa's hand tightly and smiled. "Thank you so much, young lady."

Melissa smiled back and scooted to the end of the line to wait—again.

Melissa showed compassion—burning compassion. She thought about Jesus' example, blew right past the obstacles in her situation, and then burned it home with a move that left everyone's jaw hanging.

Lots of people confuse compassion with a feeling. But compassion is the <u>action</u> that results from feelings of sympathy, empathy, pity, and concern. Just because you experience these feelings doesn't mean you have demonstrated compassion. Acting on those feelings in a way that brings a solution to the problem—now that's compassion. Burning compassion means giving up everything you have to bring about the best possible solution to the problem.

Here's another true story about compassion. Once upon a time there was a man who decided to take a long walk from

Jerusalem to Jericho. He traveled alone down the steep and curvy seventeen-mile "road" between the two cities, which dropped three thousand feet in elevation. He was just walking along, no worries, when a gang came out of nowhere and jumped him. They wanted his money pouch, walking staff, and travel bag—or else.

Fan the Flame!

Compassion isn't just a feeling—it's much more. Compassion is all about action. When you feel concern for someone, do something about it.

When he hesitated, they cracked. They beat him nearly into a coma and took everything. They even took the clothes off his bloody body. Then they ran, leaving the half-dead man on the side of the road—wearing no clothes, bleeding, and lying on the rocks in the hot sun. Not a pretty picture.

Soon a priest (chief religious kind of guy) rounded the corner, also headed for Jericho. He couldn't help noticing the poor man, and he thought, *Oh, shoot! I've read about gang beatings on this road. I better get outta here* . . . The priest warily eyed the rocky hills surrounding the road, looking over his shoulder occasionally to be sure that no one was following him. He deliberately walked on the other side of the road from the victim, hoping he could decrease his chances of being robbed as well. After he had passed the horrible scene and reached a safer area, he breathed a sigh of relief and continued his journey, thanking God for protecting him.

Not long after, a Levite (assistant to the chief religious guy) came by the same way. He not only saw the beaten man but also heard him groan and call for help. The Levite thought, *I'm already late to meet the priest in Jericho. I don't have time to help this man! Serves him right. If he were really walking with God, then he wouldn't be in this mess.* The Levite also walked on the far side of the road, not wanting to be bothered by the sight and smell of a half-dead "sinner."

Finally a Samaritan (a person most Jews thought was totally inferior) came down the same treacherous curve and noticed the man in need of help. The Samaritan's feelings were mixed. He sensed danger if he remained too long in the area. He felt rushed for time to take care of his business in Jericho. He had pity for the wounded man. He thought for a second and finally decided to act.

He slid out of the saddle on his donkey and walked closer. Seeing the man's cuts and bruises, he removed a blanket from his travel bag and tore it into bandage strips. He took a vial of olive oil and a leather pouch full of wine and used them to soak the bandages and to pour over the man's wounds. He took his time, making sure to

Check It Out . . .

God has a lot to say about compassion. Check out Psalm 41:1–2 and 1 John 3:17–18.

treat each cut completely. He lifted the man into his own saddle on the donkey, soaking his own clothes in blood, oil, and wine in the process. He took the bridle and led the donkey down the road for the remainder of his trip.

When he finally arrived near Jericho, he went to a motel and signed for a room. He took the injured man inside and tended to him all night, changing his bandages and washing his wounds. The next morning, the Samaritan had business, but he stopped at the front desk and asked the employees to watch the man. He paid enough money for the room and their trouble and explained that he would be back later to check on the man and pay even more money if necessary.

This story (a.k.a. the parable of the good Samaritan) is in the Bible. You can read it for yourself in Luke 10:25–37. It's the blueprint for living your life with the compassion of Jesus. Three basic themes really form the master plan of how to imitate Jesus:

1. You have an example already set for you. Jesus talked the talk about compassion, as in this story, and then He walked the walk. Everything He said and did is an example that you can follow. Crack open your Bible every day, jump into Matthew, Mark, Luke, and John, and see what Jesus did and said. You can't help wanting to be more like Him.

2. You've got to blow past the obstacles. Several obstacles blocked the Samaritan's way. He could have been robbed. He could have been late for some very important business. He might have even reasoned that it was a trap—that the injured man was a decoy meant to lure him into danger. He would have to replace the blanket that he tore up for bandages. Yet the Samaritan overcame the obstacles and did what he could with what God had given him. He realized that he had oil, wine, a way to make bandages, a donkey for transport, and money. Everything required to help was right at the Samaritan's fingertips. He realized he was perfectly capable of helping in spite of the obstacles.

God does not call you to do something without giving you the tools you need to do it. Read Ephesians 2:10. Every time you sense the opportunity to do good, it's a moment in time that God orchestrated deliberately for you. God has blessed you with time, energy, money, talents, and more. Use them. Ignore the obstacles. Live on the edge.

The edge can be a dangerous place, so be wise and not reckless. You shouldn't endanger your life or the lives of others in the things you decide to do. God wants you around to demonstrate compassion *tomorrow* as well as today. Talk with your parents and friends, and listen to their advice.

3. You've got to burn it home. The Samaritan could have just called the camel ambulance—that would have been more compassionate than leaving the injured man there. He could have carried the guy to the inn and dropped him off. He could have done a lot less, but he didn't. He did everything he could do.

Meeting a genuine need is never easy. Some people try to

feel good about themselves by helping a little. Burning com-passion requires giving a lot. It may mean letting go of the money meant for a new computer game so a needy child can have food this month. It may mean cancelling a trip to the mall to help someone change a tire. It could mean helping Mom clean the house when you're really not in the mood. It definitely means that you will be giving until it hurts. There will be obstacles to overcome, challenges to meet, and extra miles to walk.

Fan the Flame!

Burning compassion requires giving until it hurts.

Still interested? If so, get ready for the ride of your life. You will experience a journey of burning compassion in the life of Jesus, modern examples from people who have chosen to live beyond the casual Christian life, and hard-core chal-lenges that you can apply in your life right here—right now.

2
PEOPLE YOU DON'T KNOW

Brad was soaking in the pleasure of his newfound freedom. He was twenty-one years old, just out of college, with a sweet job. He had so much extra money that he didn't even know what to do with it. On his way home from work, he began thinking of all the things he could buy—a new car, a computer, nice clothes. He caught himself getting carried away, and he whispered a brief prayer, "God, please help me to spend my money wisely. Help me to honor You."

The words were barely out of his mouth when he pulled up to the stoplight near his apartment complex. Standing there on the corner was a pudgy man in his forties holding a sign that said, "My family needs your help." Next to the man was a small boy about ten years old. Brad groaned. He had seen people on the corner before, but now he felt guilty. He knew God was prompting him to help, but Brad resisted. "God, these guys are scam artists. He's using the kid to get sympathy, and he'll probably just blow the money on drugs or alcohol. No way am I giving him money."

Brad felt the Spirit poking him still. The light turned green, and Brad sped past the beggars. Taking a deep breath, he prayed, "Lord, show me what to do." He pulled his car into a gas station and parked it. He got out and walked back to the corner where the two stood. He introduced himself and said, "I would really like to help you, but I want to know more about your situation. I live around the corner. Would you like to come over for a minute?"

The man smiled from ear to ear and shook Brad's hand, agreeing to the invitation. Once inside, Brad listened intently to the guy's story. He had injured his foot and was out of work. He was dangerously late on his rent and risked eviction from his home. All he really wanted was enough money to cover the rent—about $250. Brad obtained the landlord's name and telephone number and called him to confirm the story. Then he wrote a check for $250 to the landlord and handed it to the gentleman. "I hope this helps," he said. "God has given me a little extra, and He suggested that I share it with you today."

Fan the Flame!

Selfishness is the biggest enemy of compassion. Sadly, we're all pretty selfish at heart. What form does selfishness take in your life? Busyness? Prejudice? Condescension? Greed? Think carefully about how selfishness shows up in your life. Are you willing to let God interrupt your plans?

Most people just ignore beggars on street corners. A few people give a dollar or two out of guilt. Once in a while, someone might cheerfully offer a crisp five-, ten-, or even twenty-dollar bill. Rarely does anyone take the time to actually listen to, understand, and help them with what they really need.

Jesus' Example (Mark 10:46–52)

Jesus ran into a street beggar once too. He was headed to the city of Jerusalem, and He was totally hung up on what He was going there to do. He knew He was walking straight into His own death, and the thoughts of what He would go through likely preoccupied Him. He was just walking out of the last major city (Jericho) that stood between Him and His goal, and He was ready to complete the journey. He would walk the same road that the good Samaritan had walked earlier but in the opposite direction. His trip was entirely uphill.

People were all around Him, shouting and doing their best to get Jesus' attention. His twelve buddies, who surrounded and protected Him, were growing weary of the constant demands of so many people. As they neared the main exit to Jericho, they breathed a sigh of relief, thinking that once they left the city walls, the crowd would thin out so they could enjoy some peace and quiet.

However, rather than getting quieter, it got louder. Much louder. A blind man, strategically positioned at the busy exchange, realized from the shouts of others that Jesus Himself was walking by. Without a thought for his own safety, he rushed into the crowd and began shouting, "Jesus! Son of David! Show me some compassion!" His cries were almost lost in the frenzy, but even the people who heard him told him to shut up and go back to begging.

"Jesus! Son of David! Show me some compassion!" The blind man continued to shove his way through the crowd in the direction he thought he should go, and this time the disciples heard him. They were so tired and ready to get on their way that they tried to shut the guy up and make him go away. All of their lives they had seen blind, smelly, dirty, lazy beggars. They were not in the mood to deal with another one today.

"Jesus! Son of David! Show me some compassion!" The bind man yelled as loudly as he could, desperate for an audience with Jesus. Finally Jesus heard his cries. He stopped cold, turned around, and asked His disciples to rescue the man from the crowd and bring him over.

The blind man, who was named Bartimaeus, couldn't believe his ears. (Notice that the disciples, who tried to shut him up, had to bring him to Jesus.) Jesus looked at the man carefully and asked, "What would you like from Me?"

No one had ever asked Bartimaeus what he wanted before. He was used to people ignoring him, taunting him, or throwing him a few pennies. He stood speechless for a moment, not knowing what to say. He fell to his knees and cried, "Jesus, I want to see. Please let me see!"

Jesus spoke, and instantly Bartimaeus could see. He couldn't believe it. He jumped up and down and turned in circles, taking in the world around him. He was completely blown away by the colors of the sky, buildings, clothes, hair, grass—everything! He screamed and shouted and ran, following Jesus all the way up to Jerusalem.

Blow Past the Roadblocks

Your agenda. You could easily argue that Jesus was a very busy man that day, and He didn't have time to pay attention to one random beggar while already fighting a huge crowd. On the surface of things, it didn't appear that Jesus had planned to heal Bartimaeus. Bartimaeus simply interrupted Him and asked for help. Jesus had to make a choice—continue with His immediate agenda or sacrifice time and plans for someone else.

You've got your own plans, your own agenda. People around you are demanding things from you; you have work to do; you have places to be. It's hectic. And on top of all that, you need some free time for yourself: to eat, sleep, hang out, go shopping, work out, whatever. Do you know anyone around you, much less yourself, who has a calendar with an entry that says, "Make a total stranger's day today"?

Let's be real. Sometimes you are so busy, you have no time to spare. But if you want to fulfill God's calling in your life to know and imitate Jesus while you walk this planet, you must have an attitude that's open to interruption of your regularly scheduled programming.

For example, let's say that while you're standing in the line to get food, you notice some kid whom you've never met fumbling in his pockets, apparently a buck short of paying for his meal. You have an extra dollar in hand, but you were planning to save it for a coffee drink this afternoon. Will you remain silent and hope somehow the situation works itself out, or will you abandon your own caffeine agenda?

> ## Check It Out . . .
>
> Can you see past someone's surface need to the real need? Jesus had a special talent for that. Read Matthew 9:1–7 to see His compassion in action.

Make plans now to let God interrupt your plans so that you can become like Him by *reaching out to strangers in need*.

Prejudice. Disabled beggars were a fairly common sight in Jesus' day. In fact, they were taking over the place. Jesus and His disciples had seen plenty—not only in Jericho that day but in other towns all of their lives. The possibility of prejudice grew every time they saw another one. Some of them were unclean. Some of them were pushy. Some tried to use guilt trips. Some spent the money they received on wine and women. Some were actually nice and simply trying to survive. However, rather than give in to any of the prejudices, Jesus chose to ignore them all and meet this beggar face-to-face to see what He could do.

Do you prejudge strangers around you? Yes, you do, and you know it. Remember, though, that the sin doesn't lie in the thought that crosses your mind—it happens when you act on the thought rather than fighting it with what you know in your heart is right. Let's say that you have been raised in a family with plenty of money and a nice house, and you even have a nice car to drive. Your friends all fit in the same mold. Then one day a new student arrives in class, and the only empty seat is next to you. You can immediately tell from her hair and clothes that she comes from the a-lot-less-money group. So do you welcome her and treat her well, or do you let your prejudice take over? Do you snub her and treat her as if she doesn't exist?

Don't let prejudice prevent you from reaching out to someone new. God has allowed your paths to cross for a purpose, and He may very well be planning for you to be the one who introduces her to Jesus for the first time or who meets a specific need in her life.

Peer pressure. Don't you find it hard to believe that out of all twelve of Jesus' companions and the hundreds of other people in the crowd, no one stood up in Bartimaeus's defense? The best we can tell from the Bible, everyone wanted the blind man to sit back down and can it. Surely a few people had feelings of compassion for the man and wanted to help, but the mob mentality prevailed and overran the crowd. Only Jesus chose to ignore everyone else. He did what He knew was right despite a ton of peer pressure.

If you are honest with yourself, you will probably have to admit that you sometimes follow the mob mentality instead of being true to yourself and your God. It's hard! You want to be accepted, so you try to please the crowd. But think about it. Is everyone accepting the real you or the fake you that you're pretending to be?

Suppose you're playing volleyball with your youth group at church. You've got ten people, so the numbers work out with five on each team. You're having a great time when in walks someone who, face it, isn't coordinated at all. He stands nearby, looking awkward and hoping someone will talk to him. Everyone on your team groans quietly and whispers, "I don't want him on our team. We'll lose for sure! Let's just ignore him." What do you do? You can worry about your "image" and be quiet, or you can think about the newcomer's feelings and ask him to join you.

When your peers pressure you into mistreating or ignoring a stranger in need, look inward to your heart. What is the Spirit prompting you to do? Follow His voice, and do what you know to be right.

Bum It Home

Bartimaeus was a beggar. He was asking for money. If Jesus wanted to show the man compassion, He could have simply given him cash and kept on going. But He didn't. He took the time to ask the blind man what he *really* wanted, and of course, Bartimaeus wanted to see. Jesus didn't give the man what he originally *wanted*; He gave him what he really *needed*. And in the end God got the credit for it.

It's easy to show a "little" compassion by meeting the

surface needs of a stranger you encounter, for example, by handing a dollar bill to a street beggar. However, if you want to follow Jesus' example by burning it home, you will have to go the extra mile. Sometimes this will mean establishing relationships with strangers in order to meet their needs on a regular basis. It might mean digging deeper into your pockets and letting go of some green stuff you were planning to blow this weekend. Whatever the case, it will call for a sacrifice.

Now that you know the obstacles that stand in your way and you are prepared to overcome them by going the extra mile, it is time to establish a regular pattern of showing burning compassion to the strangers that God brings into your life. Here are some ideas:

- Get together a group of friends, and pitch in some money each month to feed and clothe a hungry child in another country.

- Take time to get to know the new student at school or new employee at work. Invite him or her to your church.

- Ask your family to adopt one or two children in your community for Christmas by buying gifts that they cannot afford. Write Scripture verses on the gift cards that express your love for them.

- The next time you are traveling, pack an ice chest full of cold drinks for any road construction workers you might come across along the way. Tell them thanks for their hard work.

⇻ Look around your neighborhood for a widow who might need some extra work done around her house. Knock on the door one Saturday, introduce yourself, and offer to do free chores.

➡ Learn about a missionary person or family serving in a foreign country and become a pen pal. Write them, and ask how you can pray for their specific needs. Ask about what needs they may have and how you can help.

➤ The next time you hear about a disaster in some other town, state, or country, form a group or work with your student group to send care packages.

Reflect

1. Think of an opportunity recently you had to show compassion to a stranger. Why didn't you help? What obstacles held you back? If you could go back in time, what would you do differently?

2. Do you ever feel that you're too busy to reach out to people you don't know? What changes can you make in your attitude or your schedule to keep this from being an obstacle in the future?

3. Read Hebrews 13:2. What motivation does this Bible verse give for being kind to strangers?

4. What types of people challenge you with your biggest problem of prejudice? What specifically can you do to overcome these thoughts and feelings and actually show compassion to someone in this group?

5. Do you ever find yourself joining the crowd to ignore or make fun of someone you don't know? What are you going to do the next time you face this challenge?

6. Ask your friends and parents to share with you the kindest thing that they have ever done for a stranger. Use their examples and stories to encourage you to do the same.

7. What is one specific thing that you can do this week to show compassion to a stranger? Pray about it, and commit to do it before the week is over.

3
PEOPLE IN YOUR FAMILY

Imagine this. You're sixteen years old. The prom is two weeks away, and you actually have a date. Your life is cool—not much room to complain.

One day you wake up feeling not quite your old self. When you sit up in bed, the room starts spinning, and you just barely resist the urge to introduce your pillow to last night's pork chops. You lie back down and call for Mom. "I'm sick!"

Three days go by, and you seem to be getting worse. Dad takes you to the doctor, who runs a few routine tests to find out what's going on with you. You're waiting in the doctor's office for the results of the blood test, laughing at your dad's corny jokes. The doctor opens the door, and in he walks with two other people dressed in lab coats—and they aren't smiling.

You'll never forget the words that come out of the doctor's mouth. "I'm afraid I have some difficult news. The blood tests show that you are suffering from a rare form of . . ." The rest doesn't even matter. You suddenly feel sicker than ever, and you bury your face in Dad's chest.

The prom comes and goes without you. You are in the hospital, poked and prodded and tired and weak. You don't have much longer. Unless . . .

There is one possible solution. A blood transfusion from a donor with a perfect match for your blood makeup could cure you. Doctors run tests on your mom, your dad, and finally your six-year-old little brother, Eli. Bingo! He's a perfect match.

Your family huddles together around your hospital bed and says a prayer. Your parents turn and ask the little guy if he'd be willing to give his blood for you. "Eli, the doctors say that if you do, it might be enough to kick this thing."

Eli looks at you, and then at your parents, and then at the floor. He asks quietly, "Can I have a few minutes to think about it?" You and your parents agree, and Eli turns and walks out of the hospital room and down the hallway. He's gone for a few moments and then returns with a weak smile on his face. "I'll do it," he offers firmly. Everyone cries, hugs are exchanged all around, and your parents tell the doctors to make preparations for the transfusion.

The next day, Eli lies in a bed next to you as all of the needles and tubes and contraptions are set in place. "Ready?" the doctor asks you and Eli. You look at your little brother, and he looks at you. You grab his hand, and both of you nod. "Let's do it," says your brother.

A gentle hum fills the room as a nurse flips the switch. "This shouldn't take but twenty minutes. So just relax and you won't feel a thing."

Eli is unusually quiet. You look at his freckled little face and say, "Eli, I really appreciate this. You're the best."

He looks back at you and says, "Thanks." He pauses for a moment before asking, "So, how long before I die?"

For a moment you think Eli is joking, and then it hits you right in the face. Your little brother thinks that he is giving you all of his blood, and that he must die to save your life.

This illustration is based on a true story told by Robert Coleman in his book *Written in Blood*. The story really shows that you don't have to be old to show compassion to those around you. You don't need a degree in theology or be some advanced-level Christian to act as Jesus did. You can be as young or as inexperienced as Eli if, like him, you're willing to give up everything to serve others.

How would you feel about your little brother if he offered to die for you? You might find it a little harder to pick on him and a little easier to give him rides to soccer practice. Your love for him just might burn a little deeper. Without a story like this, though, sometimes it's hard to be nice to your siblings. Sometimes it's even harder to be nice to your parents. Let's face it. If you're still living at home, you see them every day, and sometimes it just gets old. You want space. You want to be out on your own. And sometimes they feel the same way about you.

So how do you show compassion to people in your family? Take a look at what Jesus did for His mom, and you may get an idea.

Jesus' Example (John 19:25–27)

Don't cheat. Did you read the passage? It's only three verses. Takes thirty seconds tops. Grab your Bible and take a look.

Picture this. It was 9:00 A.M., but already the air was hot. Mary tried her best to hold back the tears, but how could she? Her oldest son was being brutally beaten right before her very eyes, and she could only watch helplessly from a distance. She winced in horror as they ripped the clothes right off His bruised and bloody body, bringing a muffled moan from Jesus. His shoulders, back, neck, and thighs were covered with deep bruises and gashes from the flogging. The dried blood had soaked into His clothes, tearing away the scabs as they were removed. She tried to go to Him, but a wall of soldiers pushed her back and threatened her if she should try again.

Mary fell to her knees and wiped her eyes. She saw the crown of thorns on His head and the blood on His face. She stared silently but with waves of sorrow piercing her soul as they forced Him to the ground and pounded nails through His flesh and into the wooden cross underneath. Each painful cry that Jesus uttered sent feverish chills down His mother's spine. She wept uncontrollably as they lifted the cross and dropped it violently into the hole that would keep it standing until His death.

John, one of Jesus' closest disciples, was there too. He knelt beside Mary and held her close, telling her that somehow it would all be okay. He lifted her to her feet and hugged her, wiping the tears from her eyes. Together the two of them stood with their friends in a quiet huddle of disbelief.

After a few hours had passed and the guards began to relax the protective circle around Jesus and the two thieves, Mary moved a little closer. John and the others followed. She looked up at her son and thought of the agony He must be going through. She looked deeply into His eyes, and He looked back at her. She thought about the first time she

Fan the Flame!

Suffering shows what you're really made of. How do you react? When you have a migraine, do you get impatient with others? When you're beyond hungry, do you get demanding? When you've got a ton of work to do, do you tune out everyone else's needs? Notice how Jesus reacts, despite being in excruciating pain and nearing death. What an amazing example!

looked into those eyes thirty-three years earlier in a little horse stable in Bethlehem. He was so tiny and helpless. She knew what to do then. She had no idea what to do now.

Lifting His tired head, being not far from death, Jesus spoke to her. "Dear woman [a really sweet way to talk to your mom two thousand years ago], here is your son," He said, nodding at John. Mary and John knew instantly what He meant—He was telling Mary that John would be her new son after He died. Looking at John, Jesus continued, "And here is your mother." He was asking John to take care of Mary after He died and treat her as if she were his own mother.

Mary couldn't believe her ears. Even though her son was in unbelievable agony and barely clinging to life, He was still thinking of her. Mary held tightly to John, overcome with the love that her son demonstrated for her during His final moments.

Blow Past the Roadblocks

"In a minute." Have you ever said that to your parents, your siblings, or your roommates when they asked for help? No way. Not you. Never. Yeah, right. You probably say it every day. Well, guess what? It's time to put that phrase to death. Right now. Not in a minute.

Jesus had every right to be thinking of something other than His mother at the moment. He was busy *dying*, you know. He had a legitimate excuse. But He didn't let that stop Him. He gave His mom one of the very last minutes of His life to show her that He cared.

When you say, "In a minute!" to the people you live with when they need your help, you're really saying, "Hey, can't you see that what I'm doing right now is much more important than you? Back off and let me finish, and I'll get to you on my time."

When your mom walks through the door during your favorite TV show and announces that she has a carload of groceries she would like you to unload, what is your first thought? Bite your tongue. Think about Jesus' example, and hop right up and tell your mom you would be more than happy to get those groceries before the milk spoils.

Let's say your dad asks you to mow the yard while he's gone Saturday morning. You know he gets back at noon, and you'd really like to sleep late, so what do you do? You know it takes one hour to mow the yard, so you figure if you at least get it halfway done by the time he gets home, he'll be glad to see you out there. You could set the alarm for 11:30 and start at the last minute. Or you could get up at 10:30 to mow *and* edge.

Bratty little Kevin has to be at the band room in fifteen minutes or he'll miss the bus to the football game, and your parents suddenly announce that they can't take him and that you have to drive him ten miles to the junior high. You're right in the middle of a chat session with some friends on the Internet, and now this? What are you going to do? You can drag your feet, or you can smile as you grab the keys on the way out.

The point is, Jesus' example shows you that you should always do what you should at the right time for the people who are closest to you. Don't think about yourself first. Think about them first.

"I don't feel like it." Okay, this excuse is a second cousin twice removed from "in a minute." Instead of complaining that you

don't have the time, now you're saying that you don't have the *heart*. Ouch. What a way to say, "I love you, Mom."

Let's be honest now. So how many times *have* you felt like doing chores, cleaning up, loaning out your nice things, or sharing the phone line so someone else in the house can use it? Of course, you don't feel like it—not most of the time anyway. Who wants to do chores?

Do you think Jesus felt like helping His mom when He did? He was dizzy. He was thirsty. He was bleeding. He was dying. No one would have blamed Jesus if He never said anything to His mother. He was in agony. He certainly didn't feel like taking care of His mom, but He did it anyway. And do you know why? Because He had a history with her. He remembered all of the times she took care of Him, and He decided to return the favor.

Check It Out . . .

Interested in reading about someone else who set aside his issues to help the very people who had hurt him? Look at the life of Joseph in Genesis 45 and 50.

Jesus doesn't make you feel like helping your family. He wants you to do it anyway. No matter how you feel. And why? Because they are your family! You've got history. Your parents have raised you. They've bought most of your clothes and food. They put a roof over your head and gave you a room with a bed. They changed five thousand diapers before you could take care of business on your own. Like they felt like doing that!

So, get a grip. You're not going to feel like doing chores, but Jesus gave you those moments as an opportunity to show the people around you how much you care about them. Get off the couch. Step away from the computer. Put down the phone. Lay down this book if you have to, and catch up on your chores. Any questions?

"I have issues." Ah, yes. Now, this is a classic. You wouldn't use those exact words or give this excuse out loud. You save it for muttering under your breath. You use it when you slam the door or roll your eyes or talk back or stomp away. "Why should I be nice to him when he . . . ?" Hold it right there. No family is perfect. You've probably been in argument after argument with every single person in your family. There are times when things aren't right between you and your dad, but he still needs you and he still loves you, even if he doesn't say it. When your roommate spills her soda all over your car and then needs help on her homework, you can hold a grudge, or you can follow Jesus' example and help out anyway.

Now, you may be saying, "Hold on. Did Jesus ever have issues with His parents or His brothers and sisters?" Yes, and it's actually in the Bible. John 2:1–11 tells the story of a time when Jesus' mom put Him in an awkward position. John 7:3–5 talks about a time when His brothers were making fun of Him. Mark 3:21, 31–32 reveals that Jesus' entire family, including His mother, thought that Jesus was off His rocker and that they might actually have to put Him away. Yet we never hear of Jesus holding a grudge. We see only Jesus holding out His hand in forgiveness.

You've got to forgive and forget when it comes to those tough times in your family. Yes, there are probably times when they are wrong and you are right. So what? Are you going to keep score and get even? Love them anyway and forgive them, just as God forgives you every day.

Burn It Home

So far we've been talking about how to *react* to the people in your home when they need your help—sharing in the workload around the house or helping out when someone asks. However, if you really want to get serious about being like Jesus and really showing some compassion, then you need to begin *acting* and not just reacting. Choose in advance to do things that demonstrate your love, even when no one asks for or expects it. In other words, be a player and not just a water boy.

Jesus loved His mother. Everyone knew that. But His last act of compassion for her was way above and beyond the call of duty. While He was in pain, He thought of her pain. Instead of being preoccupied with His death, He thought about her life. He took care of her when no one expected it. Now, that's burning it home.

What does this mean for you? Here are some ideas to get you started:

➡ Make dinner *and* do the dishes one evening so your parents can have a break.

➤ Tell one of your brothers or sisters that you want to spend next Saturday together—just the two of you. He or she chooses an activity that you can enjoy together.

➡ Buy a greeting card for your parents, and thank them for all the things they have done to raise you so far. Do the same thing for your siblings, and thank them for always being there (even though you're tired of them *always* being there).

⤷ If you can see that someone needs help at the moment, offer your assistance before she has a chance to ask.

➡ Take the initiative to clean the house and do the chores that aren't even yours.

➤ Go to your siblings' extracurricular activities, and make them feel as if they are the most special and most loved kids around.

➔ Pray for each family member and roommate by name every single day. Ask each of them how you can pray for them, and keep checking to see how they are doing.

Reflect

1. Think about any grudges you might be holding against someone in your family. Take the time to go over each issue, and do your best to genuinely forgive. If necessary, talk to each person, and apologize for anything you may have done. Then ask God to forgive you and help you to love your family in spite of their faults.

2. Evaluate your attitudes about your work—your regular chores and those interruptions where someone suddenly needs your help. Do you do them on time, with a smile, and in spite of any other reasons you may have for shading out of it? Are you guilty of throwing out one of the excuses mentioned? Make a decision to battle and overcome the selfish feelings you might have, and let Jesus' example lead the way. See Philippians 2:3–4 for further study.

3. Make a top-ten list of things that you like about each of your family members.

4. If you live at home, do you catch yourself dreaming about the day you'll leave home? You will be gone forever one day, and it's okay to think about it, but don't let it become a way of escaping your family before your relationship is right with them. Jesus lived at home for thirty years and spent only three years in ministry. That

means He spent 90 percent of His life at home with His family while He was preparing to save the planet. God put you in your family for a reason. Thank God for each one, and learn to love and live with them before you leave home.

5. Studies show that guys will treat their wives the way they treat their moms while they live at home. Girls will treat their husbands the way they treat their dads. Think about your attitude toward your parents. Do you need to make an adjustment? Do you think your future spouse would appreciate being treated the way you currently treat your mom or dad? If not, make whatever changes are necessary.

6. Your family, like everyone else's, has problems. Your friendships will never be perfect either. However, God uses everything that happens—good or bad—for the good (Rom. 8:28). Make a list of the rough spots in your relationships and the way that God might be using them to prepare you to do His work later.

7. Pull out all of the old pictures and videos, and look at them with your family. Ask each person to share his or her favorite memory.

4
PEOPLE WHO LEAD YOU

"Mr. Kinsey?" Derrick looked up from his magazine to see a well-dressed young gentleman approaching him. "Here are your keys, sir!" the salesman said with a sly grin.

Derrick held out his hands, almost trembling, and gently took the shiny new keys into his hands. He looked at them carefully and ran his fingers over the plastic and metal.

"She's all gassed up and ready to go," the man said, pointing through the glass windows of the showroom and into the parking lot.

"Thanks!" Derrick said loudly. He had to fight the urge to run out of the showroom and hop into his new car. He walked slowly, trying to seem calm, as he made his way outside to the sleek, new black car parked against the curb. This car is sweet! Derrick thought, walking around the car and admiring every curve.

He lifted the handle to the driver's side door and swung open the door—his door—and sat down inside. He breathed *in deeply, taking in that new-car smell. He closed the door, buck-led himself in, and cranked the engine. The V-8 roared to life. Putting it in first gear, Derrick eased her out of the parking lot and onto the road. He pinched himself to see if he was dreaming. All of his life he had dreamed of owning a Mustang convertible, and now with the wind in his hair and the stick shift in his hand, his dream had come true.*

Well, sort of. Derrick knew that he didn't really own the car yet. He had to make monthly payments for five years. Derrick had used the Internet to find a low-interest car loan and worked everything out with that bank and the car dealership. According to the instructions, he should receive a payment coupon book in the mail in a few days, and his first payment would be due in just over a month.

Two months came and went, and still Derrick had not made a single payment on the car. He had received no payment coupon book, and he wasn't sure what the problem was. He called the bank that had given him his loan. After a little research, the voice on the other end of the line said, "Derrick, we never gave you a loan. You never sent in your paperwork. You don't have a loan with us." In disbelief, Derrick hung up the phone. He was positive that he had sent the final paperwork—overnight in fact. Panicking, he picked up the phone to call the car dealership to see what the people there had to say.

"Mr. Kinsey, your car is paid in full. We received the check from your bank a few weeks ago, and we're all set here." Totally confused, Derrick called the bank back, only to be told the same thing—he had never been given a loan.

A smile broke out on Derrick's face. Free car! *he thought. Then he shook his head and tried to chase the thought out of his mind. "No, there's something really wrong here. Somebody is out an awful lot of money, and he just doesn't know it."*

For the next three months, Derrick placed calls, wrote letters, sent E-mail—all to no avail. The bank asked him to quit calling, and the car dealership was getting annoyed. He placed one last call to the person who sold him the car and said, "Look, you think this car has been paid for, but it hasn't. This is my final call. Please find out what is going on and get back to me."

Finally someone from the car dealership called back. An accounting oversight by a clerk had caused the error, and the dealership now wanted its money. Technically Derrick could walk away with the car without paying a cent, but he knew he couldn't do that. He made arrangements and began paying for the car the next month.

What would you do if *your* first set of wheels could be free because of someone else's mistake? Would you walk away with the title, or would you feel obligated to pay for it? Tough call.

People who lead you—people who tell you what to do in life—don't just depend on themselves. They depend on you to do your part in the game. For example, banks tell you to make payments on your loan, but you've got to send in the money. Congress passes laws, but it's up to you to obey them. Coaches tell you to run and exercise at home, but only you know whether you're pulling your weight. Teachers hand out assignments and give tests, but whether you cheat or do the work yourself is a decision you have to make. Your employers tell you what work they want from you, but it's in your hands to get it done. All of these people have your best interests in mind, and you show them compassion when you follow their instructions and show them respect.

Jesus had to follow the leader, too, even though He was God in the flesh. He could have snapped His fingers and given Himself immunity to any rule in the book. But instead, He showed us how we should show compassion to our leaders—by honoring and respecting them with our support and obedience.

Jesus' Example (Matt. 17:24–27)

Capernaum was a nice little fishing village on the northern shore of the Sea of Galilee in Israel. Word has it that Jesus spent most of His time there when He wasn't actually out in ministry. One day when He came back from a long mission trip, He headed to Capernaum for a little R & R. He was back at the house, and Peter was wandering around town, maybe looking for some food for the disciples. Since Capernaum was a border town, lots of tax collectors lived there to make sure people coming in and out of Galilee paid the proper taxes. A couple of tax collectors saw Peter in town and headed in for the kill.

"Hey, Peter," one of them said. "You hang out with Jesus, right?" Peter nodded, trying to appear calm, but sweat began to break out on his palms and forehead. "Well, we just want to make sure that He's paid the temple tax this year. Has He? Because if He hasn't, He owes us two big ones."

Peter, always quick to open his mouth first and ask questions later, said, "Jesus always pays this tax. You had better update your records there and go find someone who actually owes you some money. Now, if you'll move on, I've got things to do." Peter gathered his things and disappeared around the corner, leaving the two tax collectors unsure of whether to believe him or not.

Heading down the street, safe for the moment from those guys, Peter breathed a sigh of relief but couldn't help wondering. *Does Jesus pay the tax?* he asked himself. *I've never noticed Jesus paying taxes before, and I disagree with that tax anyway. After all, why should each person have to pay two days' wages just to support the temple? The priests are probably using that money on themselves anyway. Why, I ought to . . .* His thoughts trailed off as he opened the door to the house where everyone was staying. Jesus greeted him first and gave him a hand carrying in the food.

"Tell me, Peter," He said as they set the groceries down in the kitchen, "if a king decides it's time to collect the taxes for the year, where does he get the money? Does he go to his own family, or does he tax everyone else's family?"

Peter couldn't believe it. Did Jesus know about his run-in with the tax collectors? Why this question about taxation? Peter knew the obvious answer and said, "The king collects the tax from all the other families in his kingdom."

Jesus nodded nonchalantly in agreement and said, "Of course, because his own family members are exempt. They don't have to pay the taxes." Peter realized that with this short little quiz, Jesus was saying that because He is the Son of God, He was exempt from paying the temple tax. Peter grinned and was about to agree loudly when Jesus continued, "However, they don't understand who we are, and we don't want to offend anyone. So, it's time to go fishing. I want you to go down to the sea with your fishing line. Cast it in and wait. Soon you'll catch a fish, and when you do, take him and open up his mouth. Inside you will find a coin worth four days' wages. Take it, and use it to pay My tax and yours."

Fan the Flame!

Do you ever think that you're exempt from certain rules? Some rules are pointless, or they just don't apply to you. Yet if Jesus obeyed even illogical laws for the sake of obedience, shouldn't you do the same?

Peter couldn't believe his ears. Jesus, the God who actually is the reason the temple was built, was going to pay those lousy collectors a tax on it? Without a word, he turned around. He grabbed his fishing line and went down to the Sea of Galilee. He threw his line in and waited for a few minutes. Soon the line began to tug, and Peter hauled in a nice-sized catch. He pried open the fish's mouth to get out the hook, and there inside was the coin that Jesus promised. Reluctantly he took it back to town and gave it to the tax collectors.

Blow Past the Roadblocks

"I don't like that rule." The speed limit, your curfew, tonight's homework assignment—all of these may be things that you flat out don't like. So what do you typically do in response? Speed? Come home late? Cheat on the paper with a friend?

Jesus had every opportunity to complain about the temple tax rule. Why should He give up two days' earnings to pay an annual tax on a building that He designed? He could have stood at the front gate to the temple and defended the right for people to worship without paying. He could have turned the tax collectors into frogs. But out of respect for others, He chose to pay the tax anyway, even though He disagreed with the rule. Not only did He honor the tax collectors, but He also taught Peter a lesson in the process. Peter learned to do the same from Jesus' example.

Suppose you are driving down the road, late for work. The speed limit is clearly marked 50 mph. You could disagree with that rule, and so you push it to 65 or 70 mph. Maybe you are fortunate enough not to get pulled over, but in the process, you are telling God, the police, and the legislature that passed the rule that they can take their rule and shove it because you've got a better idea. What if you have friends or siblings in the car with you? What are you teaching them when you speed? Rather than set them an example the way Jesus did for Peter, you're doing just the opposite and teaching them to break the rules as well. Obeying traffic laws is a very basic way that you can show compassion to the authorities in your life.

"*What does it matter as long as I don't get caught?*" The coach says, "If we're going to make state in track this year, I need you to run two to three miles each night at home. Record your times, and turn them in each week." But you're tired tonight, and you've got lots of homework. Who cares if you fudge the numbers just this once? Let's see. If you average the numbers from the previous nights and divide by . . .

Stop! Don't go there. Your coach has your best interests at heart. He wants you to succeed as an individual and as part of your team, and lying about your running isn't going to improve your abilities at all. Make time to do what the coach asks, or be honest about why you had to miss.

Jesus could have very easily avoided the rule. After all, if the tax collectors had to even ask Peter whether or not Jesus paid, they must not have known for sure. Peter already told them that Jesus paid the tax, so what would it hurt to blow it off completely? "No big deal. Who's going to miss two drachmas?" However, Jesus decided the goal of the game was more than not getting caught. The goal was to show compassion to His leaders by complying with their wishes.

Admit it. You face a hundred opportunities a day to lie or bend the rules at school, home, work, wherever. Your teachers don't know for sure who's doing your homework. Your parents aren't always positive that you are where you say you are on Saturday night. Your employer isn't watching you every second that you're on the clock. You have lots of chances to do your own thing and never get caught. However, if you are a follower of Jesus, you are *never really alone*. God is always with you, and He sees everything that you do. Doubt it? Read Psalm 139 and get a picture of what it is like to be one of God's children.

God wants you to value your teacher by doing the homework yourself. Honor your father and mother by being honest about what you do and where you go. Respect your employer by working for her as you would for the Lord. Show them that you care by always doing your best, whether you're on display or on your own.

Check It Out . . .

Real obedience means you don't just grudgingly do what you should. You do it with the right heart attitude, the right external attitude, and the right timing (when you're asked, not an hour later). What you do can mean infinitely more than what you say. Check out the Parable of the Two Sons in Matthew 21:28–32.

"What good is this ever going to do me?" Calculus—yikes! How could that possibly ever help me? I'll just get my brother in college to do this for me. What about biology? No way is that ever going to help me in life. DNA or RNA—why should I know the difference? How is memorizing this song for band going to help me get a job when I graduate?

Okay, Einstein, you've got your life all planned out, do you? How do you *know* you'll never use biology or calculus? Sorry, but no matter how smart you think you are, you have no way of knowing where God will take you in the next ten years. You have no idea what you'll need to know and what you won't. God gave you these opportunities to learn and follow instructions, and your response will show your leaders and your peers whether or not you care.

How was paying a temple tax going to help Jesus? In just a short while, the people who ran the temple were going to have Jesus arrested, beaten, and put to death. In fact, the money that He paid in taxes might very well have been part of the money later paid to Judas to turn Him in. What better excuse could you have than that? Jesus still obeyed. He still paid.

If God gives you piano lessons and you can't stand them, take the piano lessons. Try your hardest. Give it your best shot. You never know how God is going to use the piano in your future. If your homework demands dealing with dangling participles and split infinitives, learn what they are and when to use them, and smile when you do it. Remember that the people who are leading you into these wonderful activities that you love so well are watching you. They notice your attitude and your effort. When you do what you know you should, you show them respect. When you deliberately do what *you* want instead, you show them no compassion and no honor. Giving your all will get their attention. If they know you are a follower of Jesus, you're going to make Him look good too.

Burn It Home

Okay. So far if you do everything that you've just read, you're going to break even. But what about burning it home? How can you show some real compassion to the people who lead you?

Notice that Jesus didn't pay just for His own tax. He made sure that He paid for Peter's as well. Did you also notice that Jesus didn't even scold Peter for lying to the tax collectors? Peter didn't know for sure that Jesus paid the tax, but he didn't get a lecture. Instead, Jesus simply supplied the money for both of them to cover their taxes. Part of following the leader is being humble and not getting on your high horse around others who aren't following so well, even if you have every right. Jesus burned it home by going the extra mile. So can you.

Here are some ideas on how to show compassion to the leaders in your life:

➤ Once a year, give each of your teachers a card. Tell them how much you appreciate what they do, even the teachers that you just can't stand! And to avoid any accusation that you're trying to be the teacher's pet, make the cards anonymous. Do it just so that they know they are making a difference in the lives of their students. Nothing makes teachers feel better than to know they are making a positive impact.

➤ If you have a job, try this. Show up consistently five minutes early and stay five minutes late. That extra ten minutes will be obvious to your boss, who will be amazed that you care enough to go beyond the call of duty.

➪ Thank your parents for setting a curfew. Thank them that they care enough to make sure that you are home safe and sound. Let them know that you appreciate all the work they do and the rules they set to keep you on the right track.

➡ If you drive and you have some friends in your car, be extra careful to obey the speed limit to the T. If it's 30 mph, drive 30 and not 1 mile an hour over. Your friends will probably notice and razz you a little bit, but so what? Set an example. Tell them that you're just doing what Jesus would do.

➤ Do you ever find yourself in a classroom with a substitute teacher? If so, be extra careful to follow her instructions and let her know that she is worthy of just as much respect as your regular teacher. And if the rest of the students are taking advantage of her, don't be afraid to stand up and ask them to get their act together for the guest.

➡ Take a case of ice-cold soft drinks down to the local police station one afternoon, and ask the receptionist to give one to each of the officers on duty that night. Explain that you just wanted to say thanks to the men and women in uniform for risking their lives to take care of you and your community. You never know—tonight may be the very night they need that little extra encouragement to assist you in a crisis.

➤ Your pastor, youth pastor, small group leader, and other church leaders often go above and beyond their call of duty to help you become more like Jesus. Take a moment to lift each one up in prayer. Come up with a way to let them know how much you appreciate their ministry.

Reflect

1. Make a list of the main leaders in your life—teachers, parents, youth pastor, boss, and so on. On a scale of one to ten, with ten being the best, how well have you shown compassion to each one through honor, respect, and encouragement? Name one thing you could do to improve the level of compassion that you show to these people. Ask God to bless the life of each one.

2. Have you broken any rules, told any lies, or cheated in any way under someone else's leadership? If so, ask God now to forgive you and to give you the courage and strength to alter your habits and begin replacing the shortcuts with obedience. If necessary, admit to the

appropriate leaders where you have fallen short, and ask for a second chance to make restitution.

3. Each of Jesus' disciples followed Him, but each did it in his own style, and all of them messed up plenty along the way. Becoming a great follower doesn't mean giving blind obedience or seeking total perfection. Do a character study of one or more of the disciples to determine how each of them developed his own method of showing compassion to his leader, Jesus. Learn from their examples, and commit to improving your relationship with Jesus as you follow Him each day.

4. Imagine for a moment that everyone on the planet agreed to play by the rules that our country's authorities have set. No more lying, stealing, or killing. What kind of a world would we have? Would your life be better or worse? Obviously, not everyone is going to show compassion to leaders and to others by doing the right thing, but what about you? What will you do in your corner of the world to make it a better place?

5. Let's say that in ten years you are going to be so successful that you have your own company. You have one hundred employees working for you, and the harder they work, the more successful you are. Your company is expanding, and you need ten new employees. Make a top-ten list of attributes and attitudes you want to see

in your new staff. Now, take a look at your list. Are *you* the model employee for your boss now? How many of these qualities do you have? How can you improve and become a better employee?

6. Sometimes our state and national leaders can seem distant and irrelevant to our lives, homes, schools, and jobs. Who are your leaders? Can you name your congressional reps and senators for your state and your federal districts? Do you know the names of your governor and the president and vice president? Find out who represents you in your state and national government. Your government teacher or the Internet is a great place to start. Write as many of them as you can to thank them for their time and efforts. Put them on your prayer list, and make a habit of asking God to help them lead as they should.

7. Occasionally you may find yourself in a leadership role. Your instructor asks you to head up a committee. You're the baby-sitter in charge of the child. You're the head of a team project in chemistry, and everyone else must follow your lead. Watch and learn how others respond to your leadership. When they do things that bother you, make a mental note of how it makes you feel. Then when you have the opportunity to treat one of your leaders the same way, you may think twice. Also, when those under your leadership do something that makes you feel good, try to do the same sort of thing for the people that you follow.

5

PEOPLE WHO SERVE YOU

Steve was already very late for dinner with his wife, and the traffic on the rainy Tuesday evening wasn't helping him any. As he pulled up to a stoplight, he tapped his steering wheel impatiently and prayed that his wife would understand.

Just before the light turned green, Steve heard a loud pop and looked to his left. The last car making its way through the light on the cross street had just blown a tire. It was a sleek black stretch limousine, now disabled and pulled over to the shoulder just to Steve's right. The light turned green, and Steve debated his next move. He knew that the driver and passenger of the limousine were probably not dressed to change a tire. He reluctantly turned right and pulled up behind the car, figuring that since he was a mechanic and already dirty from head to toe, he might as well offer his assistance.

He told the limousine driver that he would be happy to change the tire. Steve asked the driver to pop the trunk, where he found the jack and the spare. For the next twenty minutes,

Steve swapped out the flat tire for the spare and soaked himself in the pouring rain. When he finally finished and put the old tire and jack back in the trunk, the rear passenger window opened and a man motioned for Steve to approach.

"What's your name?" the man inquired.

Steve shared his name, trying in vain to wipe the grease from his hands.

"I just want you to know that I really appreciate what you did. You've kept me on time for a very important meeting."

Steve nodded humbly and then returned to his car, mumbling to himself, "And you've made me even later to a very important meeting with my wife!" He hopped in, stepped on the gas, and made his way to the modest little home just outside town.

Steve's wife was waiting at the door, dressed nicely for dinner but tapping her foot impatiently on the floor. Steve apologized 238 times, took a quick shower, and dressed for dinner. They were late for their reservation but managed to squeeze in their dinner in time to get to the movies.

The next day Steve was working hard at the shop when his phone rang. It was his wife. "Honey, you are not going to believe this. A man just came here and asked how much we owed on the house. I told him, and he wrote a check for that amount. Is this a joke? The man said this is what he owed you for changing a tire. What's going on?"

Steve dropped his jaw and his tools and raced home. Looking at the check, Steve saw the name of a well-known millionaire and suddenly recognized the man he had helped the previous day. He grinned from ear to ear and said, "Sweetie, it's no joke.

I changed his tire in the rain yesterday, and I guess this is his way of saying thanks!"

The rich man could have sent a card or a small gift, but instead he decided to richly reward Steve for choosing to take care of his plight in the rain. He rewarded his servant with an extra healthy dose of compassion for a job well done.

Jesus' Example (Luke 22:7–14; John 13:1–17)

Jesus was unusually quiet, and His disciples sensed that something was up. They talked about it in small groups, but never with Jesus face-to-face. Jesus knew their thoughts but didn't address the issue. *They'll soon understand all too well. Right now, I just want to spend one last quality evening with them before I go.*

"Peter. John. Can I see you two for a minute?" Jesus asked quietly that Thursday afternoon. Peter and John immediately followed Jesus and gave Him their full attention. "You know, this evening marks the beginning of the Passover celebration. I would like you two to go into Jerusalem. Just as you walk through the gate, you'll see a man carrying a jar of water. I know it's unusual to see a man carrying the water since women usually do that, but you'll see him, trust me. Follow him quietly to his home. When he arrives there, tell the owner of the house that the Teacher wants to know where the guest room is so He can have the Passover meal with His disciples. He'll show you an upstairs room with all the furnishings. Go out, buy all the food and wine, and get everything ready. I'll get the rest of the disciples together and meet you there at 8:00 P.M. Okay?"

Peter and John looked at each other and nodded. "We'll take care of it," promised Peter, and off they went.

Later, Jesus arrived at the house with the other ten disciples. Jesus and His twelve followers celebrated the day that Moses led the Israelites out of Egypt and rescued them from slavery. They ate the Passover meal as the book of Exodus instructed.

When the meal was over, Jesus looked at each one of His friends. He was overcome with compassion for them and wanted to show them just how much He cared. Quietly He stood up and walked over to the wall. He took His outer coat off and hung it on a pin in the wall. Then He grabbed a towel and wrapped it around His waist. He picked up a pitcher of water and poured its contents into a large bowl. He came over to the edge of the table and knelt down in front of Andrew, Peter's brother. Everyone grew quiet, wondering what was about to happen. Jesus reached out and took off Andrew's sandals. They were nasty from walking in the city dust all day. Jesus set them aside and then dipped

Check It Out . . .

How could the Lord of heaven kneel down to wash the filthy feet of sinners? The One who had every right to be proud acted humbly instead. Read Jesus' words about serving in Mark 9:33–37.

one end of the towel into the water. Then He reached out and began washing Andrew's feet.

Several of Jesus' friends gasped. Peter was really fuming. *Only the lowest slave on the totem pole gets the job of washing people's feet!* he thought. *No way am I going to let God wash my feet.*

Jesus reached Peter in the middle of the group. Peter objected firmly, but Jesus gently insisted. Peter allowed it but fought back tears as he watched his Lord clean grime from between his toes. Jesus continued around the room, washing even the feet of Judas, who in less than an hour would turn Him over to be killed.

When He finished with everyone, the room was so quiet that they could hear the blood rushing in their own ears. Some disciples were weeping softly. Some were dumbfounded. Jesus broke the silence. "Do you see what I've done? I've set you an example. Even though you are My servants, I have washed your feet as if I were your servant. That's how you are to treat each other. That's how much humility and compassion I want you to show others. Remember, the job of washing feet isn't for some slave. It's for you."

Blow Past the Roadblocks

"*It's not* my *job.*" Ever said or thought that? "No way am I doing that—it's not my job." There are people in your life who serve you. It's their job to do things for you. People like waitresses, grocery store clerks, and bank tellers—yada yada yada. They get paid to make your life easier. So when you're out for pizza with your friends, you figure it's the server's job to pick up after you, right? Never mind the spit wads stuck to the chairs, crumbs on the floor, and spilled soda on the table. You've got to get to the movies. And since you're short on cash, you couldn't afford to leave a tip. Now this server is cleaning up a huge mess and hasn't earned a dollar for your business.

Hang on a second. One person in your group is different. She's down on her hands and knees picking up the debris from the pigs you call friends. There she is cleaning up that spilled soda and carefully picking up each spit wad before dropping them all in the trash can. And now she's reaching into her purse to leave a tip, even though it won't leave her enough for the show. Wait a minute—that's not her job! What's she doing? She's doing what Jesus would do.

Jesus was literally the last person on the planet who should have been washing feet. Back in His day, people wore open sandals around all day. By dinnertime, most people's feet were black with grime. Wealthier people hired slaves to wash their feet. Poor people washed their own feet. Nobody in his right mind would *choose* to wash someone else's feet. Yet Jesus washed the feet of every one of His friends and told them to do the same for others.

You may think that the people who serve you should serve you, and that's the end of it. False. The servants God has placed in your life need compassion too. You can do this by helping them out even when it's not your job. For example, after you finish trying on clothes at the store, put them back on the hanger or fold them instead of leaving them in a pile on the floor. When the movie is over, throw your trash away. If you come home and see that Mom is making dinner for you, offer to set the table. In other words, take every opportunity to assist those who serve you.

"They don't deserve it." Why should I show compassion to someone who can't do her job right? The food came late and the order wasn't right. My friend didn't help me, so why should I help him? If someone's dumb enough to give me too much change, then I'm going to keep it.

Fan the Flame!

It's simple to show compassion to someone who deserves it or someone you love. But how about the person you dislike? Or the person who was just rude to you for no reason? You can turn around and show compassion to them too—just as Jesus did (Luke 6:27–36).

The hope is that you rarely have an attitude like this one, but when you do, remember what Jesus did. He looked into the eyes of Judas Iscariot while scrubbing the dirt from between his toes. Jesus knew that minutes later Judas would turn Him in for thirty silver coins—the going rate for a common slave. Judas didn't deserve a foot bath from the Creator of the universe, but he got one anyway. Jesus never gave up on him.

People who serve you are going to make mistakes or treat you badly, but that's no reason to walk away. They need your compassion more than ever. If the clerk accidentally gives you an extra five, don't pocket the bonus. He'll probably lose the money from his paycheck, so offer to help now by giving back the money. If your waitress doesn't seem to be on the ball, tip her extra, and tell her you appreciate her taking care of you on such a busy night. And if your brother needs help with his chores, help him, even if he ditched you yesterday.

Every human being is a handcrafted creation of God, and even if one of them who should have served you well does the opposite, don't let it get the best of you. Take a deep breath, and show him compassion anyway.

"I'm doing what everybody else does." Do you ever notice how people treat grocery store clerks? Most people turn into zombies and spit out monotone responses while in line. "Hi, how are you? Plastic is fine. Thank you." Imagine how boring it would be to have this same conversation with eighty-five people in an eight-hour shift. Aaaargh!

Everybody in the room that night with Jesus expected a slave of the house to come in and wash his feet. Jesus broke the monotony by doing it Himself. He had the disciples' attention because He was doing something totally out of the ordinary.

Don't you like it when something out of the ordinary happens—when your boring life is suddenly changed by something new and different? Of course you do. You don't want to walk around like a zombie, and neither do the people who help you. So here's an idea. *Talk* to these people while they are helping you! Have a conversation. Make him laugh. Tell her she's doing a good job. Ask him what he wishes he were doing right now instead of standing here taking care of you.

The point is, you can make someone else's day simply by being courteous, grateful, and friendly. Most people want service and nothing else. Don't be like them. Let the people who serve you know that you appreciate them.

Bum It Home

Jesus didn't wash just one disciple's feet. He washed the feet of all twelve. He didn't pay good money for a professional footwashing slave to come to dinner. He did it Himself. He didn't skip Judas. He washed the traitor's feet too. He even washed Peter's feet, despite knowing that in the next twelve hours, Peter would sleep while Jesus asked him to pray. He would foolishly pull out a sword and cut off someone's ear. He would use those same feet to run away when Jesus needed him by His side. And to top it off, he would curse and deny three times that he had ever met Jesus. That didn't stop Jesus from doing what He did.

You are surrounded by people who serve you. Go the extra mile in offering them compassion. Washing someone else's feet never seems like fun at first, but the impact you make will be worth it.

➤ If you have a mailbox at your house, someone picks up and delivers your mail Monday through Saturday. Most likely, the same person does it every single day. How often do you think the postal carrier receives a thank-you from his customers? Now is the time for you to say thanks. Buy a greeting card, and write a note of appreciation to your postal worker. Don't put it in the envelope, or he may never notice it! Instead, attach it to the outside of the mailbox in such a way that it can't be mistaken for ordinary mail. Place a sticky note on it that explains that the attached card is for him.

→ The next time you and a group of friends go to the movies together, take along a few plastic trash bags. As soon as the movie is over and the credits have stopped rolling, pass out the trash bags to your friends, and clean up the entire theater before you leave. Leave the trash bags in or next to the trash can by the exit.

→ You or your parents are responsible for paying the electric bill each month. Instead of grumbling about all the money slipping through your fingers, insert a note of appreciation along with the payment that says, "Thanks for keeping the lights on all year!"

→ The going rate for tipping restaurant waiters and waitresses is typically 15 percent of the bill, but many people don't leave anything close to that. The next time you go out to eat, leave a 30 percent tip. You might have to order water instead of a soda or get a cheaper meal, but you will definitely get the attention of your server.

➜ The building where you go to school or work has a maintenance crew. They typically work at night when no one else
is around, and they may be paid very little. Brighten up
their shift by leaving homemade cookies and cold milk
along with a note that says you really appreciate their work.

➤ If you ride the bus, get to know your driver. Find out his
name and introduce yourself. Greet him when you get on
the bus, and say good-bye when you get off. If you ever have
the chance, take the seat behind him, and ask him what he
does when he's not hauling your carcass all over the county.

➤ You probably surf the Net occasionally and find a site
that is really cool or interesting. Instead of just soaking
up what it has to offer, find out how to make contact by
E-mail before you leave the Web site. Send an E-mail that
says you really appreciate the content, and briefly
describe how it helped you.

Reflect

1. It's time for an attitude check. When people serve you at
the grocery store or drive-through window or school
cafeteria, you probably react in one of three ways: you
complain, you're quiet, or you compliment. Complaining
gets everyone in a bad mood, including you. Remaining
quiet about the service you get is okay but doesn't get
anyone's attention. Complimenting is the way to go.

Make a habit this week of complimenting the service you get from others.

2. Why do you think Jesus chose the example of washing His disciples' feet to show them that He loved them? Why not give them expensive gifts or a big party with a cake that said "Thanks to the Apostles" or something like that? How do you think each disciple's life was changed because of what Jesus did?

3. You know how it feels to be a servant because you have parents, teachers, and maybe an employer that you serve. How have these people encouraged you to be a better servant? How have they discouraged you? Based on these instances, what kinds of changes do you need to make in order to treat the people who serve you with more compassion?

4. Do you unknowingly look down on some of the servants in your life? Perhaps you think less of the garbage collector or the sewage treatment plant operator because those are jobs that you wouldn't want to do. Jesus washed feet—the lowest possible thing He could do at the time. Perhaps Jesus is asking you to lower yourself as far down as you can go in order to serve your servants. Ask Him to show you what you can do, and be prepared to act on His answer.

6

PEOPLE WHO DON'T KNOW JESUS

For weeks Erin had felt an unbelievable burden for the girls on her soccer team. She knew that they didn't know the Lord, and He was really laying it on her heart to share Jesus with them. She prayed about it. She thought about it. She dreamed about it. She did everything but actually do it.

Late one night on the bus after a game, the team rode home after a particularly hard loss to their archrivals. They were talking over plays and trying to stay hopeful for a district championship. Erin sat in silence, contemplating the loss and her desire to witness to her friends.

Suddenly the bus braked hard, and everyone sat up to see what was going on. The girls gasped as the bus slowly wove its way through the remnants of a very recent and very major automobile accident. The police and ambulance had not yet arrived, but plenty of good people had already stopped and gathered around to offer what assistance they could. One car was upside down with one wheel eerily spinning in the dim *moonlit night. Nearby, a body lay facedown on the asphalt with a large pool of blood underneath.*

The bus driver gunned it as soon as he made his way through the trouble. The familiar mechanical hum returned as they flew down the road. No one spoke. No one moved. Everyone was too stunned by the sight. The soccer game suddenly seemed pretty insignificant compared to what the people involved in that accident were suffering.

Erin was particularly moved. She wondered, What if this bus had been a few minutes earlier, and we had all been in that crash? What if some of my friends died tonight without ever meeting Jesus? *Suddenly all of Erin's previous excuses seemed so meaningless. She knew she had to do something, and it had to be now.*

Nervously Erin stood up from her seat near the front of the bus and spoke quietly. "You guys, what we just saw has made me realize how short life is and how much I care about each of you. There is something I have to tell you before we get home tonight—before one of us ends up like that person we saw back there."

For the next twenty minutes, Erin shared her testimony—the story of how she met Jesus, and the difference He made in her life. She explained that Jesus loved them so much He gave His life for them on a cross of wood two thousand years ago. She told them about the hope of Jesus' resurrection and that they wouldn't have to fear death when it came to claim them one day. She teared up as she told them that her heart's desire was for them to know Jesus.

When she had finished her speech—a speech that she had not planned in advance and that surprised even her—she returned to her seat. No one said a word to her or anyone else for the remainder of the trip home. After they finally arrived at the high school, each teammate quietly left the bus without even looking at Erin. Great, *she thought*, they all think I'm a nut. I should have just kept my mouth shut.

"Erin," a soft voice called from behind her as she was about to get into her car. Erin turned around and saw Holli, the sophomore team manager.

"Yes, Holli?" Erin asked, wondering if Holli might scold her for bringing up religion on a team trip.

"I'd really like to hear more about what you said," Holli confided. "Do you have some time when we can talk?"

Erin's eyes lit up. "Yeah, we can talk about it. But it's cold outside. Why don't we sit in my car?" For two long hours, Erin and Holli sat in the car and talked about Jesus. Just after midnight, Holli met Jesus and became a Christian. The two hugged and said good night, and Holli promised to come to Erin's church on Sunday. Erin drove home in tears, thanking God for moving in the life of one of her friends.

Holli was so excited about meeting Jesus that she joined Erin's church and then told her sister and parents about Christ. Within a few more months, they became Christians, too, and they began coming with Holli to church.

Erin's decision to finally obey God's prompting and witness to her friends paid off big time—an entire family asked Jesus to be the center of their lives. Her example is one for us to follow. When God nudges you to share your faith, go for it.

Jesus' Example (Mark 6:30–34)

Jesus was tired, more tired than He had been in a long time. He was totally worn out because His disciples were away on a missions trip, leaving Him all alone with the crowds of people who constantly begged for His attention. Usually His friends provided a protective shield around Him, pulling Him aside when He needed rest. Now He was on His own.

He sat down and removed His sandals, rubbing the muscles in His aching feet with His thumbs. It was still early in the morning, and Jesus reveled in the quiet moment alone. Then He noticed a young man approaching. Jesus immediately recognized him as one of John the Baptist's disciples. John was Jesus' second cousin, and Jesus knew and loved him very much. It was good to see a familiar face. Jesus smiled and asked, "What are you doing out this way today? Is John nearby? I haven't gotten to see him in a while!"

From the look on the man's face, Jesus instantly knew something was wrong—very wrong. Jesus stood up, anticipating the news. The man tried hard not to break out in tears. He grabbed Jesus and held Him, breathing deeply as if to energize himself for the words he had to say. Leaning back and looking into Jesus' eyes, he said, "John is dead. King

Herod threw a party, got drunk, and promised his step-daughter anything that she wanted." The words came slowly as the man choked back the sobs. "She asked for John's head on a platter. Herod liked John but didn't want to lose face in front of his friends at the party, so he had the executioner kill him. This all happened over a week ago. We buried him and then spent our time looking for You to bring You the news."

Fan the Flame!

John the Baptist was the notorious locust-eating, "camel-flage"–wearing prophet who paved the way for Jesus' ministry. (Check out Mark 1:1–8 for more.) Jesus said that no one who has ever lived is greater than John. Strive to live your life as passionately as John lived his.

Jesus hugged His friend, and the tears came quickly to His eyes. He offered the disciple words of encouragement to take back to the others. After the man left to go back home, Jesus sat down and wept. He thought about the days He and John had together a few years ago and how both were working so hard to help people find their way back to God. Now John was gone, and Jesus felt more alone than ever. All He could think about was finding a quiet place that no one else knew about so He could rest.

He looked up and noticed more familiar faces making their way toward Him. Peter, James, John, and all of the other disciples were approaching. They were in a good mood and were running excitedly toward Jesus. Peter, as usual, spoke first. He told Jesus all about their trip—about the great things that happened and the people they had reached with the good news about Jesus. For an hour, the disciples shared stories about the trip, and Jesus patiently listened and laughed at what had happened. He encouraged the guys and told them they'd done an awesome job. "We'll celebrate later with a big dinner, but for now, let's go down to the lake and take your boat out. It'd be great to find a quiet shore where we can lie down and take a long nap."

On the boat Jesus told the disciples about John. Everyone sat in silence. Andrew and John looked stone-faced. They were very close to John and had once worked with him in his ministry. The mood changed from excited to depressed, and they were all looking forward to that quiet hillside where they could rest.

James navigated the boat to a familiar quiet place on the shore—a beautiful grassy slope far away from the nearby cities. Everyone climbed out of the boat and started up the hill but stopped at the sound of voices. Turning to their left, the disciples saw a huge crowd of people running toward them. They looked back at Jesus, who sighed deeply and fell to His knees. He had no strength and no desire to do anything but collapse, and yet thousands of people came to see what He had to offer.

Jesus looked up at them and whispered a prayer to His Father. The faces in the crowd were coming into focus now, and He couldn't help feeling a deep sense of compassion for each of them. "They are running to Me because they do not know where else to go or what else to do. They are like sheep without a shepherd." Standing to His feet, Jesus resolved, "I will be their Shepherd."

He gathered the crowd around Him and sat down in the boat to teach. The water acted as a natural amplifier and projected His voice to the thousands of people who had come to find Him. They hung on His every word, and He spent the entire afternoon telling them about God's love.

Finally as twilight approached, the disciples pulled Jesus aside and said, "Hey, get these people out of here. I thought we were going to rest. We're tired and hungry. They're tired and hungry. Let's go."

Jesus smiled wearily and said, "Remember that big dinner I promised?" The disciples nodded eagerly. "Well, I think it's time we eat."

Blow Past the Roadblocks

"*I didn't expect this.*" If you read the rest of the story in the Bible, you'll see that Jesus cooked up a dinner out of thin air—enough to feed five thousand men and probably twice that many women and children. That was definitely not what Jesus expected, humanly speaking. You can see for yourself that He wanted to find a quiet place to rest. He was tired. He needed some personal space. He'd lost His cousin and just needed some time alone. His disciples were tired.

All Jesus wanted was some peace and quiet for a few precious hours.

The opportunity to share Jesus with people who don't know Him will rarely come at a time or in a manner that you expect. Don't worry. That happens to be by design. God hits you with unexpected opportunities every day so that you'll always be prepared to share—no matter what. It's kind of like your English teacher telling you that every day there just *might* be a pop quiz on the chapters you are supposed to be reading. You can read and be prepared, or you can blow it off and hope that you won't have a test.

Suppose you're wearing a shirt from a Christian camp you went to. The shirt shows a picture of Jesus hanging on the cross on the front. While you're buying a candy bar at the convenience store, the clerk asks you what's up with that shirt. What are you going to say? You can wimp out and say, "It's just some free shirt I got from a camp last summer." Or if you're prepared, you might say, "What's on my shirt is the most amazing thing that ever happened to me. Jesus loved me so much that He decided to die to pay for my sins so that He could keep me close to Him."

So how do you stay prepared? Simple. You talk about what you're excited about. If you get a new game and it's really cool, you're going to play the game a lot and tell some friends all about it. You may even try to convince some friends that they need to buy the game and play it too. In other words, it's a viral thing. You catch the bug and spread it around. Spend your time staying close to Jesus by reading about Him in the Bible, talking to Him on your knees, and practicing what you learn every day, and you'll be prepared. For further study, read 1 Peter 3:15.

"I don't know what to do or say." That's a new whine. Come on, get over it. This excuse is so lame. Of course you don't know what to say. If you always knew what to say, you would be a robot spewing vocabulary words. God doesn't want you to skip through life like a well-oiled telemarketer, spitting out a one-way sales pitch. He just wants you to share what's on your heart when the time arrives.

Besides, do you know what you would say if someone handed you a million dollars right now? Of course not. You would be speechless. But you would still manage to say something when the time came. The same is true for sharing your faith. You may not know what to say before it happens, but you will know when the time comes.

And guess what else? You've got a secret weapon. Jesus once said that you shouldn't worry about what you will say when sudden opportunities to share your faith arrive (Luke 12:11–12). When the time does come, God's invisible presence—the Holy Spirit—will immediately pump you full of the right words to say. You'll start saying things you didn't even know were in you.

Don't worry about what to say. Just stay close to God. Practice His presence. Walk with Him, and talk with Him throughout your day so that whenever you do have the chance to start talking about Jesus, you'll be ready to let go and let God do the talking—through your mouth.

"I'll do it tomorrow." Of course you will. You'll do it tomorrow, right after you finish your homework, run all those errands you've been meaning to do, start that diet, and *maybe* write a letter or two. Listen, you've got way too much happening tomorrow, so save yourself the trouble and do it today.

Jesus had every right to say, "Hey, people. You're very nice to run miles to see Me, and you sure do look like sheep without a shepherd. But I'm really tired and I've had a death in the family and my buddies here need some time to kick back, so would you please just give us some space and try back tomorrow . . . " Nope. Jesus didn't say that. Instead, He decided to act today. Procrastination was never an option for Jesus. And when it comes to sharing your faith, it's not an option for you either.

> ## Check It Out . . .
>
> What's your role in sharing God's good news with the lost? Read God's message to Ezekiel the watchman in Ezekiel 33:1–20.

Saying, "I'll do it tomorrow," is about as bright as putting a snooze button on your smoke alarm. "Yeah, the house is on fire, but I could *really* use ten more minutes of sleep." Sorry—you snooze, you lose. God is sounding the alarm that there are sheep without a shepherd all over this planet. He's looking for a few brave souls who aren't afraid to stand up *now* to be a part of the movement. If you find yourself in a conversation with a friend who doesn't know Jesus, don't wait until tomorrow to tell her the difference He has made in your life. Talk it up now.

Bring It Home

Did you notice that Jesus didn't share God's love just with His mouth? He *demonstrated* God's love with an act of compassion that blew everybody's expectations out of the water. Jesus realized that not only did the people need God's love, but they also needed food. They were hungry! So, Jesus met their spiritual needs, and He took care of their physical needs.

When you share your faith with someone, remember to take the extra step and care for any other needs the person may have. Here are a few challenging ideas to get you started:

⇨ Your youth group could be the perfect way to introduce another friend to Jesus. The next time your group does something really cool, invite a friend who doesn't know Jesus to come along. If there is a fee, pay for your friend to go along. Tell your Christian friends and youth pastor about it and bombard the person with your praying and sharing. Your friend will have the opportunity to see that a lot of people join you in your faith in Jesus.

➡ If you or some of your friends know how to set up a Web site, create an online "tract"—a Web site that tells someone the story of Jesus in your own words. Include Bible verses, pictures, your testimony, and anything else creative that comes to mind. Add the Web site address to your signature in any E-mail you send so that all of the people you communicate with on-line will be one click away from your story of Jesus.

→ Have you ever noticed how you are attracted to people who seem to give without expecting anything in return? Generosity is a key characteristic of a follower of Jesus. You can attract a great deal of attention to Jesus if you make a habit of being generous. For example, if you play a game of football with the guys one Saturday afternoon, think about taking an ice chest full of sports drinks for everyone to grab after the game is over. Sure, it may cost you a few bucks, but your friends will be curious to know why you cared enough to buy them drinks.

↪ There's an old game that says you are never more than seven steps away from anyone else in the universe. For instance, you may have a friend who has a friend whose uncle is a senator who works regularly with the president—bang, you're only four steps away from the White House. Try playing the same game with a new twist— you're never more than one step away from Jesus. So when you're talking with a non-Christian friend, try to turn the conversation to Jesus in one step. Let's say you're talking about the latest action/adventure movie where one man overcomes incredible odds to overcome evil and save the innocent people. In one move you can compare that to how Jesus overcame incredible odds— even death—to conquer evil and rescue anyone who would simply believe in Him. Try it in your next conversation. See if you can get to Jesus in just one step.

➤ Often you watch the news and hear that a natural disaster has struck a group of people somewhere. A hurricane, tornado, avalanche, earthquake, volcano, or flood has overwhelmed the community. You can sit and watch the news and shake your head, thanking God it wasn't you, or you can decide to do something about it. Get your youth group involved and put together survival packages— small boxes of things that survivors can use. Include bottled water, nonperishable foods, toothpaste, soap, and toilet paper. Toss in a Bible and a note of encouragement that includes Bible verses sharing the love of Jesus.

➤ Get a group of Christian friends together and make a trip to the local mall, beach, park, or other hot spot of activity. Go there with one purpose in mind: to share Jesus with as many people as possible. Now, before you wimp out and skip this idea, read on. Try a variety of approaches. Take an informal survey, asking people to tell you what they believe about heaven. Then ask them if they would like to hear what the Bible says about heaven. Or grab a cup of coffee and sit down at a coffee shop in a place where someone will likely sit next to you. Strike up a conversation, and lead it toward Jesus. There are a million ways to share Him with others. You can do it. Go for it.

⇨ The next time your English teacher assigns an any-topic-is-fine paper, choose a biblical theme so that you can share your faith with your class.

Reflect

1. On a blank sheet of paper make a target with three concentric circles—a large outer circle, a medium-sized center circle, and a small inner circle. Now, think about all of the major people in your life who do not know Jesus—friends, family, teammates, fellow employees, and so on. For these people that you have *never* shared Jesus with, write their first names in the outermost section of your target. Then write the remainder of the names in the section of your target that surrounds the bull's-eye, indicating that you have spoken to them about Jesus at least once before. Set a goal to begin sharing Jesus with each of the people whose names are in the outer segment. Each time you share Jesus with one of them, erase that name, and move it one step closer to the target. Continue sharing Jesus with everyone who is not yet in the bull's-eye until the day that you can write that name right in the middle. Keep your witness target with you, and use it as a base for prayer and action each day.

2. Think about the last time you had a chance to share Jesus but didn't. What stopped you? Write down the one word that explains why you kept your mouth shut— *fear*, *shame*, *apathy*, or whatever. Ask God to help you overcome this and other obstacles that typically stand in your way, and commit to sharing Jesus at the very next opportunity.

3. Do you ever notice that you talk and act one way around your youth group and another way when you are at school or hanging out with friends? You assume that Christians will understand your God-talk and non-Christians won't, so you change who you are depending on where you are.

   If you choose to hide your journey with Jesus on a day-to-day basis with your non-Christian friends, then it will get harder and harder to share Jesus with them "when the time is right." If one of them has a problem, pray about it, and then tell him that you prayed about it. If they ask what you did over the weekend, tell them about the awesome experience you had at church. In other words, don't hide anything; let them see that Jesus is part of your everyday life.

4. If you fill a balloon with water and drop it on the ground, what comes out? Water. If you spray shaving cream inside and then smash it over a friend's head,

what comes out? Shaving cream! If you fill it with helium and then pop it with a pin, what gas escapes? Helium, of course. When a balloon is under enough pressure, it pops and lets out whatever is inside. Here's one last question: When you are pressured by suffering, what comes out? Do you get angry and bitter and start whining and complaining? Or do you trust God in spite of your suffering and let Jesus come out even more? How you respond to suffering will show people what you are made of. Jesus gave us an example of how to suffer and yet draw unbelievers to Him at the same time. Evaluate your ability to continue to walk with Jesus even when you suffer. Make a commitment to share Jesus with others in the way that you respond to difficult times. For further study, read Job 13:15 and 1 Peter 2:21.

5. When non-Christians suffer, often they have no hope to get them through their difficulties because they don't believe that God is there to help them. This is where you come in. If you choose to show compassion to one or more unbelievers while they are going through a difficult time, they will be drawn to your source of strength and want to know more. Do you make a habit of looking for and meeting the needs of people outside your own small group and church, or do you retreat into your secluded world? The people who seemed to believe in Jesus the most were the people who were touched by Jesus in their time of suffering. Follow His example, and

reach out to meet the real-world needs of others. For further study, read Matthew 25:31–40.

6. Is there anything that you do, say, or possess in your life that would cause a non-Christian to question your faith in Jesus? For example, do you listen to music that promotes a lifestyle contrary to what you actually believe? Do you ever tell or laugh at dirty or ethnic jokes? Do you spread gossip? Is your tongue free from bad language? See if there is anything in your life that would create a double standard, and ask God to help you exterminate it. Avoid every appearance of evil. For further study, read Ephesians 5:3–4.

7. Sharing Jesus isn't exactly politically correct these days. After all, explaining that Jesus is the only way to heaven immediately implies that every other "religion" in the world is false, and that makes people uncomfortable. Don't let that kind of intimidation stop you. Be bold in sharing your faith. You're just the messenger. Jesus is the One who said, "I'm the only way."

7. PEOPLE YOU CALL FRIENDS

Esther Kim and Kay Poe were best friends. They met one year at a holiday party and had been inseparable ever since. Esther's father ran a tae kwon do studio in Houston, Texas, where the girls learned the sport together.

For more than a decade, the girls' friendship continued to grow, as did their skills in tae kwon do. Though they fought each other for practice, the two were in different weight divisions and rarely faced off in official competition. They spent hours supporting and encouraging each other to advance in the games. They laughed together in the victories and cried together in the defeats.

Each of them had a lifelong dream—to one day compete in the Olympics. They wanted it badly and worked like crazy to reach that goal. They got their chance—the national trials for the 2000 summer Olympic Games in Sydney, Australia. But there was a catch. The Olympics had only two women's weight classes, so Esther and Kay would have to compete against each other for their dream. Only one of them would make it.

The competition bracket pitted the two against each other only if both reached the final match. Esther successfully defeated all of her opponents to make it to the finals and waited anxiously to see if her friend would do the same. Kay fought furiously in the semifinal match, but near the end she dislocated her kneecap. She managed to finish the round and win, but her knee was in unbelievable pain.

Esther didn't see the match itself but managed to arrive just at the end. She strained to see or hear the results and noticed Kay's father walking out of the ring. He took another step, and then she saw Kay clinging to his back, crying. Esther pushed her way through the people to be by her friend's side. She knew that if tough Kay was actually crying, she must be really hurt.

Esther arrived in the holding area at the bottom of the stairs just as Kay's father gently helped Kay lie down. She was in tears, and her knee was swelling by the minute. Not many min-utes later, Kay and Esther were scheduled to meet in the final match to determine who would go to the Olympics. With Kay injured, Esther knew that she could easily defeat her friend. But she didn't want an easy victory.

> ## Check It Out . . .
>
> Competition between friends can put a huge strain on their friendship, or it can really strengthen it. Read the story of Jonathan and David, two best friends who competed for the throne (1 Sam. 18–20).

Holding each other, the two cried for a while without a word. Finally Esther spoke.

"Kay, what are we going to do? Your knee is torn apart."

Kay shot back, "We're going to fight. That's what. Nothing changes. Nothing."

Esther didn't want to win because of an injury. It wasn't fair. She knew she had a tough choice, a choice that depended totally on her. Both girls' dreams hung in the balance, and Esther wasn't about to take the easy road. "Kay, I'm bowing out. I forfeit. You go to the Olympics. You're better than I am. I want you to go."

Kay's jaw dropped in disbelief, and she shook her head. "No! You can't do that! We have to fight!"

Esther continued, "Look at your knee, Kay! I've got two legs, and you've only got one. You can't fight me now. Only one of us can go to the Olympics. I want it to be you. You can make both of our dreams come true. You're going. That's the end of it. I've made up my mind."

Kay sobbed as she gripped Esther's strong arms. "There's no one else who would ever do something like this for me. You are such an amazing friend!"

Kay didn't win the gold in the summer Olympics. In fact, she didn't even place. But she did learn that she had something worth far more than gold—a best friend who would give up anything for her.

Jesus was that kind of friend. He had three very close friends named Mary, Martha, and Lazarus. And the day came when their friendship was really tested too.

Jesus' Example (John 10:40–11:45)

Jesus knew two things: His time was short, and He was sick and tired of the Pharisees. Pharisees were supposedly the religious people of the day, yet they were always angry and hateful to the people who needed God the most. So, He'd had enough. He needed a break. And to get them off His back, He did something no self-respecting Pharisee would ever do. He left Jerusalem and kept going until He crossed the Jordan River and had left the country of Israel completely.

Ah, yes. He finally had some peace again—it was so refreshing. With no Pharisees to hound Him, Jesus was free to reach out to people as He saw fit. Scores of people came to see Him, and He touched them with His teaching, healing, and love. The word spread. More people came. More people believed. Jesus was at the top of His game—for a while.

One day a messenger came to Jesus with disturbing news. His friend Lazarus was very sick. Lazarus's two sisters, Mary and Martha, wanted Jesus to come to their house and heal Lazarus before he got any worse. The family lived in a suburb of Jerusalem—the place Jesus had gone to such trouble to escape.

Jesus knew He had to return to Jerusalem soon, but not just yet. He told the messenger to return with these words: "Do not worry. This sickness will not end in death. This has happened for a reason—so that people may fully realize who I am."

Jesus stayed where He was for two more days and then

told the disciples, "Okay, guys. It's time to go back. Get your things together, and let's go. I want to make it to Jerusalem as soon as possible."

The disciples looked at one another and scratched their heads. Peter shook his head in disbelief. "*Go back?* Did I hear You right? Those Phari-freaks just tried to kill You, Man. You can't be serious."

Jesus smiled, knowing they didn't understand just yet. "Look. It's not like I'm stumbling around in the dark here wondering what I'm doing. I have the light of My Father to guide Me, so I'll be just fine." His voice grew softer, and His eyes gazed at the ground. "Lazarus has fallen asleep. I need to go back to Bethany and wake him up."

One of the disciples said, "Well, hey, if he's sleeping, then he'll get better. What's the big deal?"

Jesus looked back up again and said, "By *asleep* I meant that he is dead. That's the big deal. And it's a good thing I wasn't there, because you need to see what's about to happen so you will believe. Let's get going."

The men were silent as they made their way across the Jordan and into Jericho, where they spent the night. The next day, they started up the steep, winding road toward Jerusalem. The road was hard, the trip was long, and conversations were brief. Finally they arrived at Jerusalem but chose to walk around it instead of through it to get to Bethany on the other side.

As Jesus approached Bethany, word spread quickly that He was coming. Mary and Martha were in their home, grieving with friends over the death of their brother. When Martha heard that Jesus was almost there, she took off running and met Him at the city gate a few blocks from the house. She fell on her knees and burst into tears. "Lord, if You had only been here, Lazarus would still be alive."

Jesus comforted her and assured her that Lazarus would live again. Martha thought Jesus meant at the end of time, but Jesus had other plans and let her know about it. Martha ran back to the house to get Mary, who came out to meet Jesus. Everyone at the house followed Mary, assuming that she was going to Lazarus's grave to mourn. Like her sister, Mary fell to her knees and cried, "Lord, if only You had been here, Lazarus would not have died!"

Jesus was suddenly overwhelmed with grief at the sight of His two friends and their suffering. He said, "Where is he buried?" Thinking that Jesus wanted to go to the tomb and mourn, they led Him to the man-made cave where Lazarus's body lay behind a stone sealing the entrance. Jesus placed His hand on the stone, knelt down to the ground, and wept as no one had ever seen Him weep before.

A hush fell over the crowd of people there—Mary and Martha, their friends and relatives, and the disciples. Everyone assumed that Jesus was crying because He had loved Lazarus so much. But Jesus wept for much deeper reasons. He wept for reasons that could be conquered only by His own death in a few short weeks.

Jesus stood back up, turned around, and said to the men in the crowd, "Get this rock out of the way."

What? What did He say? Everyone looked at each other, back at Jesus, and then at the two sisters. Martha thought that Jesus simply wanted to look at Lazarus one last time. "Jesus, it's been four days since we buried him. You roll back that stone, and the stench will knock us over."

"Martha," Jesus responded, "I told you that if you only believed in Me, you would see amazing things from God. Do you believe Me?"

Martha nodded, her tear-filled eyes still on Jesus, and motioned for the men to roll away the stone. She was right—it stank. The smell almost made the men who rolled the stone away gag. The people backed away and covered their faces, wondering what possessed Jesus to ask for this.

Jesus said a prayer out loud to His Father. When He finished, He placed one hand on the entrance to the tomb. He took a deep breath and paused. It was so quiet that you could have heard a camel hair drop. Everyone waited to see what Jesus would do. He lifted His head, looked into the tomb, raised His other hand into the air, and said firmly, "Lazarus, come out!"

The words echoed out of the tomb and passed eerily back to the mourners behind Him. The skin on Mary's neck began to tingle, and she shivered as fear and anticipation rushed down her spine. She leaned forward to look into the tomb and then screamed as she saw the shape of a man, wrapped in graveclothes, simply walk out.

Some people cried. Others shrieked. One man ran away so fast that his feet threw gravel on his wife as he disappeared in a cloud of dust. Many fell to their knees and praised God. Everyone noticed that the smell had suddenly vanished. Jesus smiled and said, "You just don't look too good in that, Lazarus. Would someone please bring this man a change of clothes?"

Blow Past the Roadblocks

"There's nothing I can do in this situation." Do you ever feel helpless when one of your friends is going through something that you can't fix? His parents are getting divorced. She's been diagnosed with leukemia. His girlfriend dumped him. She doesn't have a date to homecoming. It's tough when you can't do anything about it.

Remember, though, that with God, nothing is impossible. Lazarus died, and that's basically something you can't do anything about. Jesus could have said, "Oh, well. That's that." Instead, He marched right into the middle of the situation, prayed to His Father, and did what no one thought possible. He brought Lazarus back to life.

Jesus did a lot more, though. Obviously the climax of the story occurs when Lazarus came back to life, but did you notice what else Jesus did? Check Luke 11:35—the shortest verse in the Bible. It's only two words, but it says a whole lot. "Jesus wept." He wept! He didn't lecture. He didn't say, "There, there, it will be okay." He empathized so much with what everyone was going through that He couldn't help weeping too.

So, there are two things to remember when one of your friends is in trouble and you feel that there's nothing you can do. First, if your friend is hurting, hurt with him. Don't spout off empty words. If she's crying, cry with her. If she doesn't get a date to the prom, tell your date that you cannot go with him, and you and your friend can go without dates together. You've *really* got to understand how a person feels if you're going to feel it with him. Listen to him. Understand him. Feel what he feels. If a friend is down in the dumps, climb over the fence and get down there with her. Let her know that her pain is your pain.

Fan the Flame!

What "impossible" situations are you facing now? What problems are overwhelming you? Remember, nothing is impossible with God (Mark 10:27). Don't underestimate what He can and will do. Take all your requests to Him in prayer, because He cares for you (1 Peter 5:7).

Second, never say never. God can do anything. Pray for your friend. Pray out loud with your friend. Grab your friend's hand, and ask for the impossible—that his parents get back together; that the leukemia be healed; that a new and better girlfriend comes along; that she gets invited to homecoming. Whatever. Don't ever let anything your eyes see or your nose smells keep you from believing that God cares, and that He can do something about the situation.

"*It's too much trouble.*" You'd really like to go to the funeral of your friend's grandfather, but it's a three-hour drive, and this is your weekend off work, and you didn't even know this guy, and your friend probably won't even notice—so you'll just ask your friend how it went on Monday at school. That should be enough.

Jesus could have thought the same thing in His situation. When Lazarus got sick, Jesus was enjoying some of the best days of His ministry. He was out of the country. The last place in the world He wanted to be was anywhere near Jerusalem, and Lazarus practically lived there. It was a lot of trouble for Jesus to pick up and come back all that way. Time, distance, and enemies all begged Jesus to stay put. Yet Jesus decided to think of His friends first and Himself second.

That's the ticket. Think of your friends first and yourself second. Don't let the opportunity to show compassion to a friend slip away because a little trouble is involved. Your friend will notice that you weren't there at her grandfather's funeral, and yes, it probably will be okay. But who wants an "okay" life? If you do go, your friend will remember it forever. She'll know that you really cared because you *did* go to all that trouble.

"*I'm giving more than I'm getting.*" Of course you are. This week the judges gave you a 9.8 for outstanding kindness to your best friend on the balance beam, but only a 5.3 to him because he fell off. You win the gold.

Every friendship goes through phases where one of you seems to be carrying more weight than the other. Don't ever base friendships on your expectations of what your friends should or shouldn't be doing. Base it on who they *are*, not on who you want them to be.

Jesus could have easily argued this point, you know. He was dodging stones and crossing rivers and healing people and teaching the truth and forgiving sin. He was altering His plans and climbing hills and comforting others. Who was there to help Him? Who cared about what Jesus was going through? He didn't ever care that He was giving more than He was getting. That is the very reason He came to earth—to give (Mark 10:45).

So don't keep score. Friendship is not a game. It's for real, and it's for keeps. Yes, it's okay to occasionally feel that you're the one doing all the giving. Shake it off. Pray about it. Remember Jesus' example. Then get back on your feet, and start giving again. God won't let you get the short end of the stick. See Galatians 6:9 for proof.

Burn It Home

Sometimes compassion in friendships seems to come easily. You don't struggle with any of the problems mentioned earlier, and you have a great time. But don't forget, you have more friends than just your best friend. And even your best friend may need more compassion than you sometimes give. If you are really willing to show some compassion, try these ideas:

⊃ Unexpected little gifts always brighten someone else's

day. Don't wait for your friend's birthday or Christmas to give something that says, "Hey, I care." You don't have to spend a lot of money. Just give something creative. You know what your friend likes. Give something that will bring a smile.

➤ Okay, so the girls liked the first idea, and the guys are thinking, *Whatever*. Here's a more *masculine* idea. Give your friends a nickname—something that makes them feel good about who they are. Even Jesus did this. He called Simon "Peter"—or "the Rock." He nicknamed James and John "the Sons of Thunder." Those three guys were sort of His inner circle, and they all had nicknames. Pick a name that emphasizes a good quality that you see in each friend.

⇨ Remember what they tell you. If you tell a friend that you are really worried about your history test tomorrow, doesn't it make you feel good after the test when the same friend remembers to ask you how it went? Being a good listener means acting on what you hear, not just nodding your head.

➡ Don't be a blabbermouth. If your friend tells you something in confidence, don't turn around and tell someone else. You can lose a friendship instantly by violating trust. You can earn and keep a lifelong friendship if you know when to keep your mouth shut.

[87]

⊃ Keep your commitments. Don't make promises you can't keep. If you say you'll be there to help paint a room on Saturday, don't sleep in. Be there early. Sometimes it's easy to make a commitment to get the good feeling of pleasing your friend now, but then blow it off later when the time comes to do what you said. Say what you mean. Do what you say.

→ Show your loyalty. Sometimes tough times will challenge your friendship. If your friend leaves over the summer to stay with a different parent, make sure you're there when school starts again. If you have really conflicting day schedules this year, make some time to get together in the evenings and on weekends. Don't be a fair-weather friend. Stay close even when it's hard.

➥ Pray for your friends. Daily. Keep a list of all of their prayer requests, and take each one to God. Periodically ask them how things are going and how else you can pray for them.

Reflect

1. The book of Proverbs has a lot to say about friends. The New King James Version of the Bible contains nineteen references to the words *friend, friends,* and *friendship.* Look up these verses, and study what the Bible has to say about friendship. You can use a concordance to find

where these verses are located, or go to www.biblegate-
way.com.

2. List your top five friends. Now, give yourself a grade of
A, B, C, D, or F for how good a friend you have been to
each of them. Don't rate yourself on how you think you
have done. Ask yourself how each of *them* thinks you
have done. If you don't rate an A+ in every case, what is
the source of the problem? Where can you improve?
What can you do differently? Be specific, and make an
action plan to improve your grade.

3. Write down the most meaningful things that your friends
have ever done for you. What makes each particular
thing so special? Analyze each one to determine why it
spoke to your heart so powerfully. Now, be a memory
maker for someone else. What can you do to make
someone else's list of meaningful things?

4. Do you ever use any of your friends? Be honest. Are any
of your friendships based on selfish things, such as what
someone else can do for you? Sometimes you can try to
make friends with someone because of what you can get
out of it. Take inventory of your friends, and be sure
that your motives are pure. If for any reason they are
not, do what it takes to set it straight.

5. Have you ever had a falling out with a friend? If you

are carrying a grudge or an attitude of unforgiveness, God wants you to fix the problem right now (Matt. 5:23–24). Work things out, and do your best to restore the friendship.

6. Have you placed limits on your friendships? You may not think so now, but if you dig a little deeper, you may discover just how much love you are willing to offer. For example, are you willing to die for any of your friends? Jesus said that the greatest love of all is for someone to give his life for his friends (John 15:13).

7. Here's a tough one. Are your friendships centered in Christ? A true friendship must have Jesus as the reason it exists and the glue that holds it together. It's very difficult to have a really close friendship with an unbeliever because you two can't share the one thing that's most important to you in life. Of course, you should love and care for unbelievers and do everything you can to help them know Jesus, but your closest friendships will really be with other Christians. Your friends should help you grow closer to the Lord rather than pull you away. For further study, read 2 Corinthians 6:14–16.

8

PEOPLE YOU CALL ENEMIES

The Central Valley Community Church ran a ministry called *Choose Life*. The small group was dedicated to ministering to women who were considering abortion. Occasionally the members would get together and go to a nearby abortion clinic, stand out on the sidewalk, and share the gospel and alternatives to abortion. They held up signs that proclaimed "Choose Life" and encouraged women to allow their babies to live. They stayed within the law and never shouted at or antagonized anyone going into the clinic.

However, a pro-abortion activist group decided to give the little church a taste of its own medicine. The pro-abortionists decided to get everyone together and picket the church one Sunday morning as worshipers arrived. They prepared signs with slogans such as "Keep Abortion Legal" and "It's MY choice, not yours."

Fortunately the pastor of the church overheard that the group was coming. So he went to the local donut shop and ordered several dozen donuts and hot coffee. He arrived early Sunday morning and set up card tables outside his church in the parking lot and along the sidewalk. He painted signs that said, "Welcome, protesters." He placed the donuts and coffee on the card tables and asked several people in his church to meet him for prayer before the protesters arrived. There he led a prayer for the pro-abortion activists and asked the members of his church to stay outside and share Jesus.

Soon the protesters arrived. They tried to picket, but were soon overwhelmed by the hospitality of the church members. They couldn't believe that their enemies were offering them donuts, coffee, and conversation. Some scratched their heads. Others took their signs and went home. Some stayed to hear the good news about Jesus. One man even gave his life to Jesus and changed what he thought completely.

If the pastor had decided to ignore the protesters, they probably would have picketed all during services and maybe even scared away potential guests. If the pastor had decided to scream, "You evil murderers are all going to hell!" he probably would have encouraged the activists to protest even more. However, his approach destroyed the protest before it started. He showed

Check It Out . . .

"Do not be overcome by evil, but overcome evil with good" (Rom. 12:21 NIV).

Check out Romans 12:14–21 to learn how God wants us to treat our enemies.

his enemies compassion, and they didn't know how to react. What the pastor did for his enemies is very similar to what Jesus did for His own enemies.

Jesus' Example (Mark 15:1–39)

"What a rotten day," Mercurius muttered as he stumbled out of bed that morning. "If only the gods would save me from such a day as this." As much as he loved the honor of being a Roman centurion and having a hundred soldiers under his command, parts of his job were awful. Like today, for example. As the commanding centurion, Mercurius had the delightful job of overseeing an execution. It wasn't exactly fun to be in charge of *killing* three men. Especially with the Roman method. Could anything be worse than crucifixion? Mercurius shook his head in disgust, dreading the task he had to do.

He didn't even like this cursed country of Israel. He'd always envisioned that being a Roman soldier would take him to new and exciting places, far-off lands that he'd never even heard of. Well, it wasn't all it was cracked up to be. This loathsome city of Jerusalem had been nothing but trouble to him. The people were all wacked-out with this bizarre religion, going around saying there's only one God. Imagine that—only one God! Mercurius had always been taught that there were hundreds of gods. The Jews were just way too fanatical.

So today Mercurius had a crucifixion to look forward to.

Two thieves and some murderer named Barabbas. Even though he hated crucifixions, he could never let his men see that. He had to watch every sick detail with a blank stare, never showing any emotion in front of his men. That's how he'd gotten his post. He was a good soldier, and everyone knew it.

When Mercurius arrived in Pilate's court that morning as ordered, he stood at attention and awaited further instructions. Much to his surprise, the court was already bustling with activity. He asked around and found out that those psycho Jewish religious leaders had finally arrested Jesus—something he knew they had been trying to do for quite some time. The vultures were petitioning Pilate for the death penalty *today*.

Mercurius shook his head in disbelief and walked outside for some fresh air. He had heard a lot about Jesus of Nazareth. One of his close friends, another centurion, knew Him. The guy raved about Jesus and even claimed that He was the Son of God. He said that Jesus had healed one of his servants by just saying one word. That seemed hard for Mercurius to believe, but this friend of his was a stable guy, not the kind to go off the deep end.

Time and again, Mercurius had promised himself that he would try to find this Jesus character, but the chance had never come. But today it looked as if he would be the one to execute Him. How ironic. Really, though, Mercurius thought that if this guy was truly the Son of God, then He could save Himself from Roman soldiers.

A messenger came quickly outside to find Mercurius. "Sir, Pilate asked for you to report at once." Mercurius turned and headed back into the court, where Pilate sat on his judgment seat. A man stood silently beside him. Mercurius assumed He must be Jesus.

"Take this man, Jesus of Nazareth, and have Him flogged the usual thirty-nine lashes. See to it that He doesn't die," Pilate said.

Mercurius bowed and then gave the command for his soldiers to take Jesus outside to the flogging post. At his instructions, two of the soldiers stripped Jesus of His clothes and chained His feet and legs to the flogging post in the outer courtyard. An unusually large crowd gathered and began to jeer. Some stared expectantly at the prisoner, obviously waiting to see if He'd pull some miracle stunt to try to get out of the situation. Jesus didn't move.

Each of the two soldiers picked up a cat-o'-nine-tails—a nasty whip with a wooden handle and nine strips of leather to rip the victim's back. Each leather strip was filled with chips of bone, glass, and rock in order to tear and bruise the flesh of the victim. Many men had died after only forty lashes to the back. Thus, the Roman custom was to deliver thirty-nine blows—just one short of death.

Mercurius reluctantly gave the signal. The soldiers took turns, lashing Jesus hard on His back with the whips. No matter how many floggings Mercurius saw, he never got used to them. Jesus cried out each time He was struck, unable to contain Himself because of the pain. Mercurius counted carefully to thirty-nine, not wanting his soldiers to get out of hand. It seemed as if it would never end, but finally he gave the order and commanded that Jesus be dressed and returned to Pilate. His back was torn open from His shoulders to His waist. Even His legs were covered in blood; blood was everywhere. He could barely stand.

Apparently Pilate had thought that the flogging would satisfy the Jews. He brought Jesus out before the crowd and said, "Here is your King! Shall I let Him go now that He has been punished?" But the crowd, incited by the Jewish leaders, began shouting, "crucify Him!" They yelled for Barabbas to be released as part of the annual Passover custom. The crowd was in such a frenzy, it bordered on being out of control. Mercurius shook his head in disbelief, watching for Pilate's reaction.

"Fine! Here He is," Pilate replied. "You crucify Him. Let the records show that this is your choice, not mine. Release Barabbas. Crucify this man Jesus!"

Mercurius stared in shock at Pilate, knowing that his last words were directed at him. After a stunned moment, Mercurius ordered his men to release Barabbas and to prepare Jesus and the two thieves for crucifixion. Each of the three men was given a large wooden cross to carry from the court all the way through the city and up the hill called the Skull. The soldiers surrounded the prisoners to keep them from escaping and to protect them from the angry crowd. Mercurius walked directly behind Jesus, not wanting to let Him out of his sight. Jesus was different. While the other two prisoners swore and screamed back at the crowd, Jesus walked silently, stumbling from weakness but pushing ahead.

At a steep rise in the road, Jesus fell to His knees, pressed down with the weight of the cross on His back. Mercurius longed to help Him but could not show any signs of weakness or sympathy. He kicked Him softly and told Him to get up. Jesus looked up at him with gentle eyes. It was the first time Mercurius had ever seen His face up close. Then Jesus collapsed to the ground.

Mercurius scanned the crowd and spotted a strong-looking man and snapped, "You there! Yes, you! Carry this cross to the top of the hill!" The unlucky stranger, Simon of Cyrene, leaned down nervously and picked up Jesus' cross. Mercurius offered Jesus a hand to lift Him to His feet.

Once they reached the top of the hill, the soldiers surrounded the prisoners, each of them anxious to have a part in the whole thing. They started arguing over who would get to hammer the nails. How sick! Mercurius always avoided that task. Each prisoner was stripped and then forced down onto his cross. One soldier stood on the prisoner's hand while another placed a nail over the wrist, just above the joint, and drove a nail through the flesh into the wood on the other side. Mercurius grimaced and turned away, not wanting to see Jesus' hands and then his feet nailed.

This method of torture caused excruciating pain in the hands and feet. The victims had to choose between placing their weight on the nails in their feet or the nails in their hands. If they chose to hang on their hands, their elbows would come out of the sockets, and their lungs would not be able to take in enough air to survive. If they placed their weight on the nails in their feet so they could breathe, the leg muscles would soon tire, and they'd have to alternate again. Back and forth, the victims would squirm and agonize until they died from blood loss or suffocation.

Fan the Flame!

The only way we can truly love those around us is if we see the best in them. We have to see past their defense mechanisms, appearance, rumors, prejudices, and failures and see them for who they really are—God's beloved children. That's what Jesus did for Mercurius, and that's what He does for each of us.

The soldiers stood at attention, facing Mercurius to signal that all three prisoners were ready. He gave the order, and simultaneously all three crosses were lifted and dropped roughly into three-foot holes that anchored them to keep them vertical during the entire execution. The drop caused horrible pain, and Mercurius watched as Jesus convulsed in agony.

Mercurius had to think of it as just a job. He couldn't make it personal. Quickly he ordered his men to form a circle to keep the crowds away. Then he had to watch. His job was finished only when all three men were dead.

He stood there silently, watching and listening to the

execution. He watched the soldiers cast lots to see who would win the clothes of the dying men. He watched the Jewish leaders smiling and laughing, so satisfied with themselves and taunting Jesus. He heard people yelling at Jesus to come down off the cross to prove that He was who He claimed to be. The thieves even joined in. Yet Jesus said nothing.

What an unbelievable person! He never seemed angry or bitter, not at the soldiers, not at the crowd, not at the religious leaders. Mercurius heard a few quiet words from Jesus as He hung there. "Father, forgive them. They have no idea what they're doing." Forgive them? Mercurius stared in amazement at Him, wondering how Jesus could forgive him.

Suddenly it became dark. Not like a cloudy, overcast sky. It was pitch dark at high noon. The crowd grew quiet. The taunts stopped. Everyone looked nervously around, wondering what was going on. One of the thieves seemed to believe in Jesus' power. The Jewish leaders started to go home. Mercurius watched the scene, not knowing what to do or think. He was supposed to be in control.

Jesus lifted His head and cried out in a loud voice, "It is finished!" His body fell limp and motionless on the cross. Immediately an earthquake shook the ground violently, and Mercurius fell to the ground. People screamed and ran in panic. The soldiers tried to hold their position, even though they were frightened.

For the first time in his life, Mercurius didn't care what anyone else thought. He knew that Jesus was who He had claimed to be. He had never seen anyone like Him before.

Overcome with emotion, he shouted, "Surely this man was the Son of God!"

Blow Past the Roadblocks

Gut reaction. Think fast. What would you do if an authority figure walked in and accused you of something you didn't do? Would you quietly explain your innocence, or would you scream and shout? What you do in a moment of confrontation like this is your gut reaction. It can be good or bad, right or wrong. How you react is your choice.

Jesus went through more suffering the last night of His life than anyone could possibly imagine. Many times during His suffering He was hit suddenly and unexpectedly with taunts, blows to the head, hair pulled from His beard, or nails driven through His flesh. In each of those violent situations, His gut reaction could easily have been a harsh word or a return blow. Instead, He remained quiet, even calm. No matter what happened to Him, Jesus immediately reminded Himself that every event on this earth is under God's control, and even though it may be evil, God will make something good come of it. This attitude is called *meekness.*

Exhibiting this attitude is not easy to do. You don't just become meek. You have to practice. Before the time comes to express your gut reaction, you have to make a habit of reminding yourself that everything, whether good or bad, will work out for good because you are a child of God (Rom. 8:28).

So when someone accuses you unjustly of something you

didn't do, hold back any evil reactions of anger. Remind yourself of Jesus' patience and humility, and respond the same way He did—in meekness.

Prejudice. Prejudices don't hit suddenly, like a gut reaction. You learn over time to be prejudiced against certain people. Prejudice means you prejudge someone before you know the whole truth. For instance, if you see a person of a certain race steal a car, you might foolishly assume that anyone else of that race is a car thief. Stupid, right? But how many times have you prejudged someone because of skin color, the clothes he wears, the friends she has, or the part of town he lives in? Prejudice is rampant in our society.

Jesus was challenged by prejudice in His society too. Some Romans thought Jews were religious idiots, and some Jews thought that God hated all Romans. Jesus could have assumed that the centurion in charge of His execution enjoyed the torture, but for all we know the centurion couldn't stand playing a part in Jesus' death. Prejudice requires *assuming*, and Jesus had made up His mind that He wouldn't assume anything. He simply loved and forgave everyone equally.

You are faced with prejudices every day, and you know it. You see someone and make a snap judgment and *boom*— you're prejudiced. It's ingrained in your head. Somewhere along the way you started assuming that certain kinds of people were worth less than you, and you deliberately avoid them. Well, guess what? You don't know squat. You *can't* know. God didn't give you the privilege of reading other people's minds, so you can't make any judgment unless you're just lazy and start assuming. Don't assume. Just love. Learn to accept people for who they really are and not for what you think they might be. Practice putting away prejudice.

Hate. Hate is an emotion that can be described only as the opposite of love. If you love someone, you want the best for her. If you hate someone, you wish the worst. You find yourself fantasizing about hurting or even killing your enemy. Typically if you hate someone, you justify it by pointing out something that this person did or said to you. "He called me names." "She stole my boyfriend." "He left my mom and me." You figure if someone hurts you enough, then you have a right to hate that person.

If that line of thinking is true, then Jesus had a right to hate just about everybody. Judas became an enemy when he sold Jesus' life for a few silver coins, but Jesus still loved him. The Jewish leaders lied and held illegal trials to put Jesus to death, but He never hated them. Pilate had Him flogged and ordered His crucifixion. Roman soldiers taunted and beat Him. People shouted names and jeered. Thieves cursed Him. In all of that, Jesus loved them anyway. He even asked His Father to forgive them.

Is there anyone in your life that you actually hate right now? Did you know that it is impossible to be a follower of Jesus and to hate someone at the same time (1 John 2:9–11)? If you hate someone, you have to walk away from Jesus because He is pure love. Being away from Jesus is no place to be. It's dark. It's dangerous. It could be deadly. So stay close by Jesus' side, and practice loving the people that you call your enemies.

Burn It Home

We don't know exactly what made the Roman centurion choose to become a believer there at the foot of the cross, but you can probably bet that it had something to do with the absence of hate—and the presence of love—in Jesus' final moments. It blew that soldier away, and he realized that Jesus was for real. If you want to be authentic and help other people know the Jesus you know, practice loving your enemies, not hating them.

➜ No one likes to be on the receiving end of a jeer. It's hard not to throw one right back. The next time someone makes fun of you, surprise her by offering a genuine compliment in return. If she fires back another taunt, return with another praise. You'll win this contest every time. She'll be so confused, she'll probably just walk away. See Romans 12:14.

➢ If you drive in traffic, you may discover new enemies every day! The guy who cuts you off. The girl who tailgates. The older man driving 30 mph in a 55 mph zone. Guess what? God intends for you to learn something from them: patience and compassion in spite of the circumstances. So wave at the guy who cuts you off. Move over if you can to let the tailgater go around. Back off the older man, and thank God for a few more minutes of prayer time in the car. It's hard to get angry behind the wheel if you're talking to God along the way.

➥ Sometimes your parents are wonderful, and sometimes you get so mad at them that you do things you shouldn't—for example, roll your eyes, talk disrespectfully, ignore them, or throw a fit. As easy as it is to do at the time, expressing your anger in these ways is not the answer. Think about it. If your parents tell you no, do you think yelling about it will change their minds? Instead, take a deep breath. Sit down. Explain that you are really trying hard to accept no because you wanted a yes, but that you are willing to do what your parents ask. After they take your temperature to see if you are sick, they will be a lot more likely to listen to what you have to say, and they might even reconsider their position.

➪ If you come from a divorced family situation, sometimes a person you don't know is suddenly spending a lot of time with you. Mom has a boyfriend. A stepsister is moving into your room. If you're not careful, this newbie can become an instant enemy. Remember, though, that the new person doesn't know what to think of you either. You can prevent a whole lot of hardship if you do your best to show compassion first. God allowed this new person's life to intersect with yours for a reason.

➤ Even if you forgive an enemy, he may continue to bring hardship to your life. What then? The Bible says to pray for your enemies (Matt. 5:43–47). Translation—tell your Daddy about it. Ask God to give you relief from the trouble. Then ask God to help your enemy be so convicted about the pain he is causing that he will turn to God and ask forgiveness.

→ Sometimes one of your friends becomes an unexpected enemy. She tells one of your secrets. He takes your girl. She lies about you. He steals your money and denies it. Whatever the case, you have a reason to be fighting mad. You can't control what your friend does, but you can control what you do. Keep on being nice, showing compassion, and calling her your friend. Even on the night that Judas sold Him out, Jesus called him His friend (Matt. 26:46—50).

→ When you're playing sports, whether one-on-one or on a team, you may have a tendency to think of your competitor as your enemy. Show good sportsmanship. Do your best to be the winner, but if you lose, be the first to congratulate your opponent on a nice move or on a good game.

Reflect

1. Make a list of your current enemies, from worst to least. Put the person you can't stand the most at the very top of your list. Next to each name, write down the reason for your hatred. Now, stare hard at each person and each reason. Forgive them all. Then ask God to forgive you for hating. If you find this difficult to do, that's okay. But stick with it until you can honestly say that

you have forgiven each one. Then crumple up the piece of paper and throw it away.

2. What is your typical gut reaction to someone who does something you don't like? Are you more likely to smile and wave, frown and pout, or throw punches? On a scale of one to ten, with one being "I love you and it shows," and ten being "I hate you and I want to kill you," where does your gut reaction of anger typically fall? Work hard at moving your number closer to one this week.

3. The Bible says that being angry is okay, but you need to remember a couple of things when managing your anger (Eph. 4:26). Don't sin when you're angry. In other words, if someone hurts you, you will probably get angry, but you don't have to channel that anger into revenge. And don't let the sun go down on your anger. In other words, make a habit every day of taking your anger to God and laying it at His feet. Then walk away, and let Him worry about it. Trust Him to take care of the things that anger you.

4. Make a list of your prejudices. A sample list might include a certain ethnic group, the jocks, or older people. Where did these prejudices start? What can you do to overcome them? Make a commitment now to work at destroying each prejudice and replacing it with compassion.

5. What happens when you have an enemy that you forgive

once, but he gets in your face again? How many times should you show compassion to this jerk? Peter once asked Jesus the same question, and Jesus said, "Forgive him 490 times a day" (Matt. 18:21–22). That means this person can hurt you once every three minutes for twenty-four hours straight, and you are *still* supposed to forgive. Is that possible? Do you think Jesus meant literally seventy times seven, or did He mean "all the time"? Does it seem that you are constantly trying to forgive and not to hate someone in your life? Don't give up. Keep forgiving. Keep showing compassion.

6. Though you may not actually *do* anything to someone else who hurts you, Jesus says that even *thinking* hatred toward other people is as bad as murdering them with your bare hands (Matt. 5:21–24). The temptation to think evil toward someone else will always be there, but you can decide not to entertain those thoughts. The next time you feel like strangling your little brother or running your car over that enemy, hold that thought— hold it over a cliff and drop it. Let it go. Then replace it with a kind thought toward that person.

7. Is it possible that you are someone else's enemy? Is there anything you have done to cause someone else to want to hate you? If so, do whatever is necessary to make things right with this other person.

19

PEOPLE WHO NEED FORGIVENESS

Gideon's shoulders lurched involuntarily with the clanging sound of the large steel door behind him. This was it. He was inside an actual prison. He couldn't believe it. Here he was, only seventeen years old, and he now stood in the heart of the slammer. Fortunately he was there to help lead a Bible study in the prison chapel and not to be an actual inmate.

The Clemens Unit in south Texas was a medium-security prison with about one thousand inmates. The average age of the inmates was nineteen. Their crimes ranged from armed robbery to murder. Gideon was totally surrounded with high-level security—the outside fence lined at the top with spiral razor wire, the walls of the prison itself, two levels of steel doors, and finally the interior hallway. To Gideon's surprise, many inmates clothed in dirty white uniforms walked freely around him.

He stayed close to his friend Phil as they were led through the hallway and into the chapel, trying not to stare at the hardened faces of criminals the same age as they were. He breathed a sigh of relief when they reached the chapel doors and walked inside.

Gideon, Phil, and two other leaders held a brief prayer meeting with the chaplain and then set up to form two small group Bible studies for the inmates. Soon, the fuzzy-sounding intercom announced to the inmate population that the chapel was open for one hour to anyone who wanted to attend. Any inmate not in lockdown or solitary confinement was free to join.

The chapel doors opened, and fifty men slowly poured into the room. Gideon was nervous, not sure what to say to the men. He stared at the floor and pretended to be getting ready, but inside he was very unsure of himself. He finally noticed what appeared to him to be the youngest man in the room, about seventeen as well, and walked over to begin a conversation.

"Hey, how's it going? My name's Gideon." He stuck his hand out as a friendly gesture.

The prisoner shyly shook Gideon's hand and replied, "Name's Mike."

An awkward silence ensued, and Gideon wasn't sure how to continue. Not knowing what else to say, he said, "So how long are you in this place?"

Mike shuffled his feet and looked back at Gideon and said, "That's a nice jacket, man. Is that your school jacket?"

"Yeah," Gideon mumbled, suddenly ashamed to be wearing something nice from "the outside."

"It's a cool jacket. I like it." Mike paused, then continued, "I'm in here for life, man. I'm seventeen years old, and I'll never get out. I killed somebody."

Gideon felt as if the blood in his body simply stopped moving. He had just shaken hands with a murderer. His skin began to tingle a bit, and his whole body felt cold. Mike was staring at the ground, waiting for a response from Gideon, who was now trying very hard to find the right words to say.

"You know," Gideon began, "I just got this jacket a few weeks ago. It's my senior year. I go to high school about ten miles from here. Where are you from?"

Mike smiled, glad to see that his newfound friend hadn't run away in fear. The two briefly shared their stories of growing up, told a few jokes, and shared a few laughs. Gideon was surprised to see how easy it was to overcome his fear and befriend a killer. He realized that only Jesus inside could give him that kind of peace and strength.

Soon the Bible study began, and Gideon shared Jesus with the group that had wandered into the chapel. The twenty-five or so in his group included more murderers, thieves, and rapists. All of them wanted to know more about God and His forgiveness. "In this place," one of the inmates said, "you will die from guilt if you don't get the forgiveness that God brings."

Prison inmates aren't the only people who need forgiveness. The mother who stepped out of the bathroom to answer the phone while her baby fell forward in the bathtub and drowned in one inch of water longs for someone to say that it's going to be okay. The friend who has become addicted to Internet pornography is dying inside to find freedom from his guilt. The girl who just slammed the door on her mother and said she hated her doesn't know how to turn around and say how sorry she is. The father who abandoned his children ten years ago agonizes over how to return and seek their love once again.

It's very easy to write these people off. "You blew it. You do the crime and you do the time. Sorry, Charlie. Away with you. Out of my sight." As you will soon see, however, Jesus' attitude toward even the most evil people was quite different. Instead of running away, He decided to get a little closer.

Jesus' Example (John 8:1–11)

She knew it was wrong, but she told herself it was her right. *I deserve this*, she thought. *My husband doesn't care about me. He's wrapped up in his work. He never takes me out anymore. I know he's cheating on me. Fine. Let the thunder roll.*

Mariah covered her face extra carefully as she made her way through the city streets. She deliberately chose noon as her time of travel—the hottest part of the day when most other women were at home tending to their families and homes. Only a few people on business bustled about, and Mariah avoided their gaze as she turned the corner down a narrow street.

Fearful that she was being followed, she zigzagged and looped through the city streets, pretending first to head toward the marketplace and then the temple. Finally when she was sure that no one knew who she was or where she was going, she made her way toward the rendezvous point.

She looked in both directions and knocked anxiously on the door, her heart pounding half from shame and half from excitement. The door creaked slightly, and she saw him. He smiled. Her husband *never* smiled at her like that anymore. Her shame melted away. She took his hand. She went through the door. She fell into his arms.

She became lost in his hold as they made their way to the back of the one-room home. He whispered words that loosened her will. She took off her hood and let down her hair. She was ready to give herself completely to him.

Fan the Flame!

No sin is so great that God cannot forgive it—not even murder. In fact, God shows off His grace by using forgiven murderers in His plan. He chose one to lead His people out of Egypt (Ex. 2:11–15) and another to spread the gospel to all the world (Acts 7:54–8:1).

Crash! The once dimly lit room was suddenly filled with light from the open door. Mariah jumped up and screamed as six shadowy figures marched inside and grabbed her violently. "Adulteress!" one of them shouted. "God will punish you for what you have done, you evil woman. You have broken His law, and now you must die." Two of the men held down her lover as the other four rushed her outside and down the street.

Once her eyes adjusted to the bright outside lights, she could see the men who held her. They were Pharisees—the religious leaders of the Jews. They read and carried out God's Word. She knew they were right. The Bible stated plainly that any man or woman guilty of adultery should be executed. She looked over her shoulder for signs that her lover would come and rescue her, but he was nowhere to be found. She cried uncontrollably as they dragged her through the narrow streets, passed astonished onlookers who could now see her face clearly. Her captors shouted, "Make way! Move yourselves! This woman is to be executed for adultery!"

Mariah slumped in the arms of the Pharisees and begged for mercy. One of them slapped her and told her not to speak. Her life was over. She knew it. Her husband would know. Her neighbors would know. And soon, they would stand her up against the wall in front of everyone and throw rocks at her until she died.

Through her tears, she could see that they were climbing the steps to the temple. The other two men had caught up with her, and all six carried her through the temple entrance and into the outer, open-air courtyard. Up ahead, a large crowd was gathered around a man named Jesus, listening to His teachings. The Pharisees interrupted with their shouting and accusations and demanded a hearing with Jesus. The crowd parted, and they made their way to the wall where Jesus stood.

As the Pharisees caught their breath, murmuring and pointing spread through the crowd. They shoved Mariah harshly toward Jesus. She stood trembling, trying desperately to find a way to hide her face from the onlookers. The leader of the Pharisees spoke. "Jesus of Nazareth, we just caught this woman in the very act of adultery. You and I both know that the law teaches plainly that such a woman is to be put to death. Well? What do *You* say we should do with her?"

The crowd grew immediately silent. All eyes flashed back and forth between Jesus and the woman, waiting to hear Jesus' reply. What would He say? The Pharisees figured they had Jesus between a rock and a hard place. If He said to kill her, as the law required, then His message of kindness and love would seem to contradict itself. Yet if He said to let her go or give her a lesser sentence, He would be violating the very law that He claimed to teach. Either way, they figured that Jesus would look like a fool in the eyes of the crowd, and they could finally bring Him down.

Jesus looked at the woman, then at the Pharisees, and then at the crowd. Finally, and quite unexpectedly, He knelt down on the ground. *What's He doing?* everyone thought. Skeptical eyebrows rose, and everyone stood on tiptoe to see what Jesus was up to. Jesus reached out His hand and began writing something in the dirt on the stone floor of the temple. He said nothing. He simply wrote.

Whispers ran through the crowd. "They've stumped Him!" one person said. Another followed, "He has no idea what to do." Similar opinions continued to resonate. The Pharisees began to smile and relax. *We've got Him!* they thought.

They spoke again, this time more boldly and with more flair for the crowd, "Jesus of Nazareth, great Teacher of the law, You who once said that You came to fulfill the Law and the Prophets. How do You respond? Are You speechless? Are You clueless? What should we do here? The law is quite clear. The law says that this woman deserves death. Look, the rocks and the witnesses are here. Shall we begin the execution?"

All during this time, Jesus continued to write something illegible in the dirt with His finger. Mariah stood, frozen in place, afraid to even move. Jesus stopped drawing and reached over to pick up a large rock and then rose to His feet. He set the rock at the feet of the Pharisees. Everyone held his breath to hear Jesus' answer.

"Take this stone," He began. Mariah's spirit sank as she braced herself for the news. The Pharisees grinned. The eyes of the people in the crowd grew as big as saucers as Jesus continued. "Take this stone, and if any one of you is without sin, let him be the first one to throw it and begin the execution."

With that, Jesus knelt back down and continued writing on the ground. For the first time, Mariah looked up. She looked at the stone and then at the Pharisees. The crowd now focused attention on the men who had brought the woman. They stood motionless. Their smiles were gone, and now the pressure was on them. Seconds, then minutes passed. The Pharisees looked at each other and then over their shoulders at the crowd. Finally the leader of the Pharisees—and also the oldest in the group—simply turned around and walked away. A few seconds later, he was followed by the next oldest member in the group. This trend continued until the youngest Pharisee sheepishly made his way through the crowd and left the temple courts.

After all of them had left, Jesus stood again to His feet. Mariah was overwhelmed simultaneously by guilt and by relief. Jesus walked over to her and put His hands on her shoulders, facing her toward the astonished crowd. "Woman," He said aloud, "where are your accusers? Is there no one here to condemn you?"

Mariah trembled. Between sniffles she managed to utter, "There is no one, Sir."

Jesus looked up toward the crowd and stated softly, "Then I don't condemn you either. Now return to your home and leave your life of sin."

Blow Past the Roadblocks

"It's their own fault." Why should you care about prison inmates? After all, they knew what the penalty for their crimes was before they committed them. And what about the father who abandoned his children and now wants back into their lives? His kids have every right to tell him to hit the road.

Jesus had every right to condemn the woman caught in adultery. The law didn't waver on adultery. If you were found guilty, then you paid for it with your life. In fact, the same finger that wrote the law against adultery (Ex. 31:18) wrote in the dust before pronouncing sentence. The woman made her choice. She knew the consequences. It was her own fault.

Jesus could have immediately ordered her execution, but He didn't. He refused to condemn her. Instead, He forgave her.

It may very well be that someone in your life has committed a heinous crime—either a crime in the eyes of the law or an act that hurt someone you love very much. You have a choice to make. You can hang on to the anger and demand some form of punishment, or you can open your heart as Jesus did and forgive. That prison inmate needs someone who cares to forgive him for his crimes and tell him about the love of Jesus. That deadbeat dad who asks for mercy needs to know that there is hope for the future.

Practice forgiving. It's not the easiest thing in the world to do, but it is what Jesus would do. He's already done it for you. Why not do it for them?

"It's not my problem." Let's say you see someone in your school hauled off by the police for drug possession. You don't know him. He's a loner, just another face in the crowd. This is his problem. Not yours. Forget about it.

> ## Check It Out . . .
>
> No matter how much someone else hurts you, it's nothing compared to how you have hurt God. But God completely forgives your sin, and you too must forgive others. See Colossians 3:13 and Matthew 6:12 for more details.

Not so fast. Jesus could have easily dismissed the woman as "not my problem" too. He could have said, "You read the law correctly. So go ahead. Take her outside and stone her, and let Me get back to teaching here." Instead, Jesus made this woman His problem. He came to her aid. He defended her. He saved her life. He took away her guilt and challenged her to live better.

Just because someone doesn't sin against you directly doesn't mean that you should avoid getting involved in showing her forgiveness. That druggie needs someone to show up in the juvenile detention center tomorrow and tell him about God's love. The woman you read about in the newspaper who fell asleep at the wheel and killed her husband in a head-on collision needs to know that there is forgiveness.

You can shrug your shoulders and shake it off as someone else's news, or you can jump in, get involved, and spread God's forgiveness around. Strangers need forgiveness too.

"*I can't forgive* that." Child molestation. Murder. Rape. Drunk driving. Abortion. Homosexuality. *No way am I forgiving that kind of stuff. Give the guy the injection. Put her away for life. I hope they catch AIDS.*

If those kinds of thoughts have crossed your mind, then you've placed limits on God's forgiveness. As hard as it is to imagine, God loves child molesters, murderers, rapists, drunk drivers, homosexuals, and abortion doctors. We often forget that He loves all of His children the same, you and the rapist. He cares about them before, during, and after their crimes or their sins. He would *never* get in their faces and scream hate, as so many "Christians" like to do. Instead, Christ would offer forgiveness and challenge them to leave their lives of sin—just as He did for the woman caught in adultery.

Christ showed compassion to even the worst of sinners. And He calls us to do the same. No matter what the sin, we are to love the sinner. That shocking expression of compassion will remind lost people that there is a God who loves them, a God who longs to bring them back into His arms. When we show His love, people are irresistibly drawn to Him. It is God's job to judge or to forgive, not ours.

If you know a girl who prematurely ended the life of her unborn child, the last thing she needs is condemnation. She needs to see the powerful love of Jesus. And she needs to see it from you. If you know someone caught up in homosexuality, yeah, you know it's wrong, but that's not your problem. Your job is to show compassion to the guy, not alienate him. If everyone else treats him like a person with leprosy, well, how will he ever find his way to Jesus? Step in and treat him as Jesus would—with loving compassion. It's the most attractive, healing force on earth.

Remember, compassion doesn't say, "Oh, it's okay. Go ahead with what you're doing. No big deal." Compassion says, "You know what? What you did is very wrong. But I won't be the one to judge you. I'll lead you to the One who forgives." Just as Jesus did, you should encourage lost people to seek His forgiveness and to leave their sinful lifestyles.

Bum It Home

You're just getting started. In addition to forgiving others, you need to give them what comes afterward—love and encouragement and restoration. Jesus not only forgave the woman; He also forgave her in front of her accusers. He affirmed her in front of a crowd that could have condemned her. He went beyond the law and offered love. So when you forgive someone, don't just wipe her slate clean. Write some new, good stuff on it, and sign your name at the bottom. Here are some ideas to get you started:

- Have you ever seen your dad treat your mom unfairly? Or maybe your mother isn't being so kind to your father. If you're not careful, you can start tucking away resentment inside until it builds up and explodes. Forgive your parents for their failures, and pray for their marriage. Ask them to tell you about the time they first met and when they decided to tie the knot. Let them know that you're glad they got together and have you.

- Gossip is an easy way to spread unforgiveness beyond your heart to others. "Did you hear what she did?" "That guy had the gall to . . . " Don't *ever* make conversation with stories about the sins of others. If you are part of a conversation that starts heading in that direction, change the subject or say something that's actually good about that person.

- Sometimes the hardest things to forgive are unintentional acts. Your sister ruins your favorite dress. Your best friend finds herself pursued by the guy you have a crush on. Your dad misses your ball game because of traffic. Sure, it hurts. But don't make these people suffer because of something that was unplanned. Let them know that you forgive them and you still love them.

➥ If you're involved in sports, sometimes it's easy to get angry with one of your teammates because of a bad play. She cost you the game, so you fume. Hey, she already feels guilty for letting everyone down, so be the first to be by her side and let her know that it's okay.

Reflect

1. Just because someone hasn't sinned against you directly doesn't mean that you should avoid being involved in offering forgiveness. Think of people around you who may have committed a crime or caused an accident that would make them feel guilt. What can you do to show them that you and God care and are willing to forgive?

2. Vigilante justice is the idea that people have a right, in extreme cases, to take the law into their own hands and punish someone who commits a crime. Have you ever heard of any particular cases of this kind of so-called justice? Do you think this kind of justice is right? Why or why not?

3. Make a list of the sins and crimes that are, in your opinion, the worst of the worst. What makes these things worse than others? Do you know anyone personally who is actually guilty of any of these? Have you forgiven the person? Don't let the sins on your list become a stumbling block. Learn to forgive everyone, even the individuals who make your list.

4. Read Matthew 7:1–2. What is Jesus saying? Think of someone whom you judged harshly in recent days. Now, imagine God judging you the same way for *your* sins. It's a scary thought, but God says that the way you choose to judge others for their sins is the same way He will judge you. In other words, if you want God to give you some slack, cut everybody else some as well.

5. The two sins of abortion and homosexuality are legal in our society. How do you think Christians should approach women who seek or who have had an abortion? How should we treat abortion doctors? What about gay and lesbian couples? Hating or yelling isn't a solution, but neither is condoning the sin. So what should you do?

6. The death penalty is a hotly debated topic. Do you think Christians should support or oppose the death penalty? Does supporting the death penalty mean you are unforgiving? Do you think that a man or woman facing exe-

cution is more likely to seek God's forgiveness in the final hours? If so, does that make it a good thing? Do you think victims' families should have the right to witness an execution? No matter which side of this issue you choose, make sure that your goal is that the death-row inmate receives forgiveness—from people and from God.

7. Forgiveness brings freedom to everyone involved. When you are forgiven, you are freed from the guilt that hangs over you. It's an awesome feeling, a total relief from your burden. But there's the flip side too. When you forgive others, you are freed from the bondage of holding a grudge. What does it feel like to finally forgive someone who wronged you? Who do you think "owes" you for treating you wrongly? Sometimes we can go for years without forgiving the people we should, and do you know which person it really hurts more? The person who's eaten up inside by holding a grudge. Examine your heart, and ask God if you need to forgive anyone.

10

PEOPLE WHO ARE SICK

Darrell and Mike were on their way home from the movies on a narrow, two-lane country road. The van in front of them was cruising a little too slow for Darrell's tastes, so he decided to pass. He looked quickly to make sure it was clear and then zipped into the other lane. Halfway past the van, Darrell realized that they were approaching a sharp curve. He decided he could make it and floored it.

Just then, a car coming the opposite direction rounded the curve. In desperation, Darrell veered his car onto the opposite shoulder, but when his tires hit the loose gravel, he started to spin. Mike grabbed the dashboard to brace himself, and Darrell tried his best to regain control, but it was too late. They were thrown back onto the highway, directly into the path of an oncoming car. In an instant, it was over.

Darrell was killed immediately. Mike's injuries were so severe that he lapsed into a coma. The doctors said there was little hope for Mike. Even if he did survive, they said he would likely be a vegetable for the rest of his life.

Mike's youth group at his church didn't like that answer. Though each of them had prayed individually for Mike, tonight they decided to band together. After Sunday night services, Mike's friends decided to stay at the church instead of going out for pizza. They sat down around a table, joined hands, and went to God together as a team to fight for Mike's life.

Mike had been in a coma for nine days. His prognosis was very bleak. His cranial pressure was rising—a dangerous sign. His friends didn't care. Instead, they took Mike to Jesus in their prayers. For nearly an hour, they took turns pleading with God to allow Mike to live. Every prayer was different, but each one was significant. Near the end of their time together, the group fell silent. After some quiet prayer, the friends suddenly opened their eyes and looked up at the same time. It was as if God had said, "Enough. I've heard your prayers. I will do as you ask."

At that same hour at the hospital, Mike's cranial pressure

Fan the Flame!

So often, we do not receive because we have not asked. We set our sights too low. We ask God for only a little when in reality, He's willing to give us so much more. Don't underestimate the Father. Remember, He's God. He wants to give us even more than we could ever want for ourselves.

suddenly stopped rising. Soon after, it began to fall. His vital signs began to improve. His strength returned. Four days later, Mike opened his eyes for the first time in two weeks. He was alive. He was well. His brain had suffered no permanent damage.

The doctors were amazed but simply credited Mike's sharp improvement to the human body's ability to survive. Mike's friends knew better. They knew that Mike had recovered for one reason—because they took their friend to Jesus in prayer.

Miracles like this one can and do happen. However, many times people forget that God is capable of healing any kind of disease if He so chooses. There is no substitute for taking a sick person to Jesus. Just ask these four friends who did the same thing.

Jesus' Example (Luke 5:17–26)

John, Saul, Nathan, Andrew, and Bart were inseparable. They had grown up together in a small fishing village along the Sea of Galilee. Like most other men in the village, they took up the business of fishing when they were old enough to strike out on their own. They went in together and bought a seaworthy fishing boat with all of the latest and greatest nets and holding tanks. They dreamed of the hours they would spend together on the water, laughing and working hard to make ends meet for their families.

Nathan was the natural leader of the group. He oversaw the fishing business—taking care of the finances and making sure each man received his fair share every week. John was the "net keeper." His job was to clean and repair the nets. Bart enjoyed the maintenance of the boat itself— seeing to it that the sails were in good shape, sealing the holding tanks for the fish, and inspecting the vessel meticulously for signs of wear. Andrew took care of the supplies— fishing bait, food, drinks, and so forth. Saul had a knack for knowing when and where to fish. He thought like the fish, and most of the time he led the group to good catches.

Together they made the perfect team. For two years they grew their business and became the top-selling fishing business in the region. Then, something happened—something no one expected. Nathan was traveling on a business trip when a group of Roman chariots in a playful race came around the corner. Nathan quickly stepped out of the way, but the wild race went beyond the road and one of them struck Nathan at full speed. He was thrown off the road and down a steep incline. His neck snapped in one painful instant, and he lay helplessly on the ground. Two other travelers saw what happened and rescued him, but Nathan was in bad shape. He was paralyzed from the neck down.

When Nathan's friends heard the news, they rushed to see him. Nathan's wife was busy tending to him, but she cried helplessly as they arrived, not knowing how she would survive with a man who couldn't even feed himself or get up to go to the bathroom. Saul, John, Andrew, and Bart entered the small house and sat next to Nathan, doing their best to console him. They talked for some time and then left—wondering what would happen to their friendship and to their fishing business as a result of this tragedy.

The four friends did their best to continue their business, but soon things began to fall apart. They started fighting over the money they earned and who deserved how much. They lost several of their contacts for selling the fish to market because the buyers assumed that Nathan's paralysis was a curse from God. No one wanted to be anywhere near a man whom God had cursed. Nathan's friends didn't know what to think. They were sometimes forced to choose between continuing their friendship with Nathan and feeding their families.

One day, Nathan's friends decided to pay him a visit and discuss the fishing business with him. They sat in his house and told a few jokes before getting to the heart of the matter. "We need business advice, Nate," they began. "Things just aren't the same. No one's buying our fish. They say you are cursed. We're short on cash. Our families are hungry. Tell us what we can do."

Nathan, who lay on a mat on the floor, turned his head toward each of his friends. "Have you guys heard of a man named Jesus?" he asked. The friends looked at each other and nodded, mumbling something about His reputation as a traveling mystic. "Well, look," Nathan said, "this is what I need from you. Jesus is traveling through town this morning. I hear He is at that big house on the other side of the village. I want you to take me to Him. I think He can heal me."

Bart spoke up first, "Nate. We don't have time for that.

Our fishing business is falling apart. This Jesus guy may be a nut for all we know. We've got to be able to sell our fish, man."

Nathan replied quickly, "Guys, you are my only friends in the world. I'm helpless here. I'm not going to spend the rest of my life lying here like a dead fish. If you want my help, then I'm asking you for yours. Take me to Jesus. Then I'll give you all the advice you want. Please . . . for me."

Nathan's friends looked at each other, remembering all of the good times they had had together. It broke their hearts to see their friend unable to move even a finger. Andrew chimed in, "Yeah, let's do it. Maybe this Jesus guy is for real. If He is, then Nathan can walk back to the boat with us!" Soon the others became excited.

Even Bart jumped on board. "Let's do it!" he shouted. The four reached down, each taking a corner, and lifted Nathan's bed mat into the air and over their shoulders. They sped out of the house, leaving Nathan's wife speechless at the doorway.

Nathan's body bounced helplessly on the mat, and several times the men had to stop and rest. Eventually they saw the crowd up ahead and realized that they had found the place. They ran faster and faster, finally reaching the house itself. There were so many people, though, that they didn't think they could get inside. They set Nathan down, and Bart ran around the whole house, looking for a door or even a window that would allow them access inside. He returned and said, "Nothing doing. There must be more than a thousand people around this house. We can't get anywhere near Jesus."

Undaunted, Andrew said, "Look. I don't care what it takes. We're getting inside the house."

Saul said, "Hey, people are just like fish. They swim in schools. Everyone is down here trying to get into the doors or look in the windows. No one is on the roof. Let's get him onto the roof."

"The roof?" everyone asked in astonishment. "There is no way to get into this house from the roof, you idiot!"

Saul smiled and said, "Not yet there isn't. Come on!"

The crew pushed through the crowd. Working together, they managed to get everyone up on the roof. Saul walked to the middle and said, "Okay, now based on the layout of the house, we are directly above the living room. This is where we go in. This roof is pieced together with tiles, so the way I figure it, we've got to tear out a hole from here to here. That will cost us some money to repair. Is everyone in?"

They looked at each other and then at Nathan. Nathan smiled and nodded his head. That was all they needed. Down on their knees they fell and began ripping away.

Below in the room, people were sitting and standing all around Jesus as He spoke. He was in midsentence when suddenly dust began to drift to the floor and sunlight appeared from nowhere. Everyone moved away from the commotion and looked up. Tiles fell onto the floor. The hole became bigger. Finally Nathan's mat appeared as his friends lowered it as far as they could through the opening. Shouting for assistance, they called for the people below to take Nathan and lay him on the floor.

The owner of the house began to shout, "What is the meaning of this! Look what you have done! Who's going to pay for that?"

Jesus silenced him with a smile and looked up at the four friends, who were looking breathlessly through the hole in the ceiling. Jesus knew exactly what they wanted. He could see the faith in their eyes. He looked down at Nathan and said, "Nathan—your sins are forgiven, every last one of them."

Nathan felt chills run through his body. He knew he was a sinner. In fact, most of his life had been devoted to pleasing himself. A wave of guilt shot through him, but it mysteriously vanished as quickly as it had come. He looked up at Jesus and realized that here was more than a mystic; this was God in the flesh, granting him forgiveness for his sinful life. Nate was overwhelmed with a longing to know Him more.

> ## Check It Out . . .
>
> The prayer of faith (James 5:15-16; Matt. 21:18–22). The prayer for God's will (Mark 14:32–36). The persistent prayer (Luke 18:1–8). The thankful prayer (Phil. 4:6). The humble prayer (Matt. 6:5–15). The bold prayer (Heb. 4:16).

Around the room, so-called religious leaders began to grumble. "Only God can forgive sins. Who does Jesus think He is—God?"

Jesus knew their thoughts, so He brought them out and into the open. "Look. Aren't you even concerned about this man? He's completely paralyzed, for crying out loud, and all you can think about is your religious rules. You are correct in saying that only God can forgive sin. You also know that only God can heal. You don't believe that this man is forgiven because you can't see the forgiveness, but to prove it to you, I'll show you something you can see."

Turning to Nathan, Jesus said, "Get up. Pick up your mat, and walk out of here on your own two feet." Fire shot through Nathan's body. Instantly he felt his hands and feet. He jumped up to his feet. His friends began to shout. Nathan praised God, thanked Jesus, pointed at his friends with a smile, and picked up the mat that had held him captive for so many days. With that, he made his way through the crowd and walked out on his own two feet.

Blow Past the Roadblocks

"Miracles don't happen anymore." Does the sign on heaven's door read, "Out to Lunch"? Are the stories in the Bible there to make us feel good about what God *used to do* or to teach us what God *can do and still does*?

There are three main reasons why you might find it difficult to believe that God still performs miracles. First, you live in an age when scientific reasoning is the ultimate "god" of truth. If you can't see it or prove it from the laws of nature, then it must not be true. When a so-called miracle comes along, you dismiss it as false, or you attempt to find a reasonable explanation for it.

Second, if you've never seen a miracle before, then why should you believe or expect one now? You might believe that a miracle can happen, but you think it won't happen in *your* lifetime.

Third, it is unfortunate that shysters have staged miracles on television that made you extra skeptical of any supernatural working of God. You don't want to be identified with the wackos, so you steer away from anything to do with miracles.

These are three valid points. However, think about this. Let's say that a storm tonight washes away a bridge that goes into and out of your town. Shortly after the collapse and long before the news has reached the authorities, you decide to drive to your friend's house across the river. It's dark outside, and as you near the bridge, a man flags you down to tell you that the bridge is out. "Whatever!" you say, blowing him off and driving by. That bridge has been there for as long as you can remember. It's made of steel. The storm wasn't that bad. You've driven over that bridge a thousand times.

Looking up ahead, you can see the bridge. Your headlights reveal the stripes in the roadway. Everything looks perfectly normal. Besides, you've never seen that guy before in your life. Why should you believe him? So, you start across the bridge.

What you don't realize is that the bridge washed away only in one section—and it happened between the stripes. The man who tried to stop you lives under the bridge and saw it happen with his own eyes. You've driven across this bridge all your life, but you've never driven on air. As you start to drive across, the roadway disappears from underneath your tires, and you plunge into the icy river.

In this analogy, you used the same three excuses to refuse to believe the truth. Your understanding of the science of this bridge made you think it was impossible that the bridge was out. Your familiarity with this bridge made you comfortable with how it used to be instead of how it is. Because you didn't know the man, you had no reason to believe him.

The paralyzed man and his four friends had the same obstacles. The doctors of their day probably told them that once a paralytic, always a paralytic. They had never seen a paralyzed man walk again. The friends had seen fake magicians come through town. They had no reason to believe that Nate could be healed. But they decided to take a chance with Jesus. They believed in spite of the doubts.

You can too. God created nature and all of its laws. If He wants to change the rules temporarily, then He can do it any time He feels like it. God is also bigger than you are. He can see things outside your experience that you can't. So don't trust your experience. Trust God. These bozos on television who make money by faking miracles for the world to see— shrug them off. They will one day stand before God to answer for that crime. Don't let their trickery make you doubt. God still works the real miracles for those who ask Him.

And that's the key. You have to ask. You have to believe. If you know someone who is sick, whether she has a cold or she has been given twenty-four hours to live, you can take her to Jesus and know that He has the power to heal her.

"It's too much trouble." You're right. Getting off your behind and down on your knees takes work. Calling some friends to meet together for prayer means pressing all those buttons on the phone. Talking to God instead of your boyfriend is sheer agony.

Get a life—a prayer life. Praying alone or with a group isn't hard, and you know it. All it takes is one person (you) who is willing to go to God for the sake of someone who is sick. The paralyzed man had four friends who had plenty of reasons *not* to take him to Jesus. He was heavy. The trip to the other side of town was long. They had business they needed to be doing. They didn't know what they would find or whether the whole idea would even work. But did you notice that they went anyway? They cared enough about their friend to take him to Jesus. Jesus could have said, "Hey, I'm in the middle of something here. Could you wait outside like everyone else?" Jesus also decided to drop what He was doing and reach out to the man.

When you hear about someone else getting sick, it's easy to say, "I sure hope she gets well." You *hope* she gets well. What if you were sick? Would it comfort you to know that people *hoped* you would get better? What you really mean is, "I don't have the time to be burdened with your problem right now, so if I just happen to think about you during my busy day, I'll *hope*."

Turn your hope into prayer. Don't just hope for this person to get better; *ask* for this person to get better. Ask God to step in and do something about it. Ask by yourself or with a group of friends. Don't let anything else stop you from taking this person to Jesus in prayer.

"I've already done everything I can." Okay, so you've prayed. You've asked God two whole times to heal this person. You've been to see him in the hospital. You even sent a nice card. Thanks! Now you can go home.

Don't give up. Keep asking. Keep praying. Keep going to the hospital. Keep sending cards. Those four friends could have easily given up when they saw no way of getting into the house. The doorways were jammed. The windows were blocked. They couldn't even see Jesus, much less get to Him. Instead of calling it quits, they decided to try something different—and it worked.

If the person you are praying for is still sick, don't call it quits. Keep doing what you have been doing, and then try something else. If you've been praying alone, start praying with other people. If you've already done that, then do it again. Just because your answer doesn't come immediately doesn't mean God isn't listening. Keep asking until you do get an answer.

Burn It Home

The paralyzed man had some great friends. Not only did they care for him, listen to him, and tote him across town; they also went through the roof. Someone had to answer for that. Someone had to pay for that. What would people think? What if Jesus wasn't even there when they dug through? In spite of the obstacles, they threw caution to the wind and did everything it took to get their friend in front of Jesus.

Jesus took an extra step too. He didn't just heal the paralyzed man. He *forgave* him of his sin. Jesus was just as concerned about the man's soul as He was his body. When Jesus heals, He heals the physical *and* the spiritual parts of you.

Here are some ways that you can imitate Jesus and the four friends to offer compassion to people who are sick:

⇒ Make a list of the people you know who are sick. Write down each person's name along with the problem. Prioritize the list by putting the sickest person first. Now, go over the list, and take each name to Jesus, asking for total healing.

➤ If you have a friend who is sick, she needs to know that you haven't forgotten about her. While you wait on God's healing, encourage her with regular visits, calls, cards— anything you can do. Keep her spirits up, and let her know that God is going to take care of her.

⇨ If you haven't already, get a group of people together to pray for someone who is sick. Jesus loves to see His children working together. Just as a rope is stronger because it has many strands, so your prayer is stronger when you get many people to agree. See Matthew 18:18–20.

➠ If you become sick—whether a simple cold or a life-threatening problem—call on your friends to come and pray with you. Ask them to see you through this whole thing, no matter how long it takes.

→ Sometimes a sudden need, such as a car accident, requires sudden prayer. Don't delay when the opportunity arises to pray for someone in this situation. Time is of the essence. Drop what you are doing. Call your friends. Form a prayer vigil. Do whatever it takes to take this person to Jesus while you still can.

Reflect

1. Do you believe that God still heals people who are sick? If so, what makes your faith so strong? If not, why not? Identify any specific doubts, and pray that God will help you overcome them. Discuss your skepticism with a Christian friend, and see what he or she has to say.

2. Sometimes after you have prayed for someone to be healed and you don't see the answer right away, you feel like giving up. Remember, though, that God always hears your prayer *instantly* (Jer. 33:3). There are often many reasons for the delay. In Daniel 10:1–14, you can see that Daniel prayed for three weeks for the same thing. An angel arrived to answer the prayer and explained that evil forces had detained him for twenty-

one days—exactly three weeks. So, when you pray, pray it through.

3. Praying for miracles in the lives of the sick is tough. You have to donate time, overcome doubts, and remain persistent. Often your faith suffers. To increase your faith, read Psalm 78. Count the number of miracles that God performed for His children as He led them to safety, despite their disbelief. Let these words encourage you to continue believing and trusting in God to answer the prayers that you have been offering.

4. Sickness is often used as a litmus test to prove either that God does not exist or that He does not care about people in this world. How could a loving God allow people to suffer? What is your answer to that question? In Jesus' day, everyone assumed that if someone suffered from sickness, then God must be angry with him. Jesus' own disciples asked Him about this issue. Read His answer in John 9:1–7.

5. Without realizing it, you may have a faith that believes that God can do little things but not big things. For example, do you believe God can cure you if you have a common cold? What if you get pneumonia? What if you get a fatal disease and the doctors say you will die? If your answer to the first question was easier than your answer to the last, then you have some growing to do.

God can heal any disease, no matter what it is. Read Psalm 103:1–3.

6. Okay, you've prayed. You've prayed alone and with your friends. You believed. You gave it your all. Now you're standing over a casket and looking down at the face of the person you prayed for. What does this mean? Didn't God hear you? Doesn't He care? Should you just give up and never pray again? Though God can heal any disease, sometimes He doesn't. Maybe God simply chose to heal the person by freeing her from her diseased body. Maybe He has a bigger faith lesson He wants you to learn. We know that God doesn't see things the same way we do. He always sees the big picture. Whatever the case, this shouldn't change your prayer for the sick in the future. Don't give up! Read Luke 18:1 and Isaiah 57:1–2.

7. If you are sick and God has not yet chosen to heal you, don't be discouraged. God knows what He is doing with your life, and He has great plans for your life. Keep praying for healing, but trust God in the meantime to use you and give you strength. See Jeremiah 29:11–13.

11

PEOPLE IN YOUR CHURCH

Lisa's church wasn't doing so hot. There was a big fight going on between two groups. One group, mostly the younger people, wanted to have drums and electric guitars and new music in the Sunday morning services. The other group, mostly people over fifty, wanted only organ and piano music. They wanted to sing only old hymns. Pastor Charlie found himself caught in the middle, doing his best to meet the needs of both groups.

Lisa, a member of the youth group, was deeply troubled by the tension in the air. She also wanted to have newer music on Sundays, but she didn't want to hurt the feelings of people who had different tastes. She had often overheard her friends making fun of "those stuffy old people," and it bothered her. Lisa had once sung a solo on Sunday morning—a peppy, newer song—and an older person had written her and chastised her for being "so irreverent in God's house."

Pastor Charlie tried his hardest to bring both groups together, but he found it a very difficult task. Key leaders in both groups refused to budge. When the pastor asked both sides to support their positions with something from the Bible, they would take verses and passages out of context to try to prove they were right and the other group was wrong.

On one particular Sunday night, the church called a business meeting, meaning that instead of just holding worship services, the members would discuss upcoming plans and vote on certain issues. At the meeting, the pastor proposed the plan that he thought would meet the needs of both factions within the church. He suggested that because the church was so packed on Sunday morning, and because different people enjoyed different styles of music, they should hold two services. The traditional service could meet first, followed by a more contemporary service. In this way, both groups could have a worship service tailored just for them rather than the current style of blending the two—a process that seemed to make both groups even more uncomfortable.

The call came for open mike—where anyone could share his feelings about this new idea. For a few minutes, everyone was quiet. Everyone shifted restlessly, unsure of what to say in an open forum. Finally a younger man stood up. "I think this is a great idea. I'm looking forward to singing something besides old hymns."

An older woman shot to her feet in protest. "Those 'old hymns,' as you call them, were written by great men and women of faith. They have much more substance to them then those wishy-washy, so-called worship songs you people have been shoving down our throats lately."

Lisa put her head into her hands. The pastor was trying to

keep a smile on his face. The large sanctuary was completely quiet. The conversation between the church members finally continued as one of the youth teachers stood.

"If anybody's shoving, it's you folks over there," he said, motioning his hand toward the left side of the sanctuary where the older people gathered. "The worship songs we like are straight out of the Psalms—you know, in the Bible. Your songs talk about God. Our songs talk directly to God. And what's with this monstrous organ fetish of yours? That is the lousiest instrument I've ever heard. No one listens to organ music in the twenty-first century. We need some instruments that people actually like."

Lisa's blood began to boil. She began to pray harder than she had ever prayed before. She felt the need to respond, but how could she? She was only sixteen years old.

The inevitable retort from the other side of the church came when a founding member of the church stood and said, "You listen to me, young man. As I see it, we over here have been in this church longer than you people over there. It's our hard work and our money that put this building here. If you want your loud, ungodly music, then by golly you can go to some other church."

The older people broke out into applause. The younger people began murmuring and making faces. The pastor stood, frozen in his tracks.

Lisa could handle it no more. She stood to her feet and asked for the microphone. "Listen to us!" she cried. "We're supposed to be a church family, and instead we're at each other's throats." The murmuring stopped as Lisa continued, "Nobody disagrees that Jesus is Lord. Nobody disagrees that we should worship Him and share Him in our community. Just because we disagree on how to worship and reach people doesn't mean that we have to fight about it. I, for one, think both sides are wrong tonight. You've been hateful to each other. You've said things that you don't really mean. If you don't mind, let me ask you a question. How many of you have honestly spent time praying about this? And I don't mean praying that God would let you have your way. I mean praying that God would do what He wants to do in this church, even if it means doing things that you don't particularly enjoy."

Fan the Flame!

Too often we are distracted by the trivial issues in our churches. We lose sight of the ultimate goal: giving glory to God. Take the focus off what you want and start thinking about what God wants. Ultimately, that's all that matters.

Hearts began to soften as Lisa carried on. They knew she was right. "We're supposed to be one. Jesus prayed on the night before He died that we would be one. Right now we are at least two. I don't think we should make a decision tonight. Instead, I think each side needs to ask forgiveness and begin understanding what the other side really wants. I think we need to stop sitting apart from each other and join hands, fall to our knees, and pray with each other. Once we start loving each other and praying with each other, then we can make a Spirit-led decision on what to do about the kind of music we use on Sundays."

With that, Lisa broke into tears. As everyone watched, she walked across the church to the older man who had just told the younger half of the church to go somewhere else. She gave him a huge hug, then grabbed his hand, and led him to the prayer altar at the front of the church. There they both dropped to their knees and began praying. The pianist took the cue and began playing softly. The pastor said simply, "She's right. She hit the nail on the head. We need to follow her example." With that the pastor knelt down with Lisa and the other man and began praying.

Soon, people began leaving their seats from both sides of the sanctuary. Older people prayed with younger people. People who felt one way prayed with people who felt the opposite. God's presence became stronger. Warmth entered the room—a warmth that had not been there for a very long time. Tears fell. Prayers rose. And finally, God smiled as the rift in His church began to heal.

Unfortunately, this sad tale is being repeated in churches all over the country. Sometimes the issue is music. Sometimes it's what version of the Bible to use. In some cases, it's what color to paint the walls. In every case, it's ridiculous. God doesn't want fights in His church. He wants a family. He wants a group of people who listen to and follow Him—together.

Jesus' Example (Acts 1:1–2:47)

Jesus stood with His disciples and about one hundred other followers at the top of the Mount of Olives just outside

Jerusalem. He had been appearing to them in various places for forty days since His resurrection from the dead. His mission was nearing the finish line. He sighed contentedly as He looked over the people He loved so much, and He prepared His final speech. Everyone had just finished the noon meal and looked expectantly to hear what Jesus said.

"My dear children," Jesus began, looking each one of them in the eye as He spoke. "You've been with Me the past three years. You've seen the miracles. You've heard My teachings. You witnessed My death, burial, and resurrection with your own eyes. You know that My purpose for dying on that cross was to freely offer forgiveness to others. You—this group right here—are now My chosen instrument to change the world. Listen carefully to what I am about to say, because the rest of the world needs to know what you know."

He continued, "Go back to Jerusalem and stay there. Don't move a muscle. Wait. Wait patiently. You will soon receive the Gift that I've been telling you about—the Comforter. The Holy Spirit, My Father's very presence, will soon come out of the sky like fire. He will fill you with power like you've never known."

Ever willing but rarely understanding at first, the disciples asked, "So are You going to free our country from the Roman government now so that we can become God's nation again?" They didn't understand that God had a very different plan.

Jesus was quick to respond: "My Father will take care of all of that in His time. As for you, go to Jerusalem and wait.

When the Spirit arrives, you will know that it is time to begin spreading the Word—starting first in Jerusalem, and then working outward to Judea, then on to Samaria, and continuing until you reach the very ends of the earth."

The words had no sooner left His lips than His feet left the ground. He extended His arms toward them and smiled as He continued to rise. Finally He disappeared behind a cloud. Everyone stood there, speechless, wondering if something else was about to happen. After a moment, they suddenly noticed that two men were standing in the group—two men who had not been there before. Angels.

"What are you looking at?" they asked. "Jesus is

> ## Check It Out . . .
>
> God never intended for His church to be divided. In fact, the very first church refused to be distracted by petty debates. Check out Acts 2:42-47 to catch the vision, and notice how richly God blessed them.

gone for now, but He will return one day—to this very spot—in the same way that you've seen Him go. But for now, you have work to do." With that, the two men vanished.

Jesus' followers looked around at each other, wondering what to do next. Finally Peter spoke. "You heard the man. Let's get going. To Jerusalem, where we will wait!"

Several weeks later, as the same group prayed in the upstairs room where Jesus had once washed the disciples' feet, it happened. Old and young, rich and poor, tall and short prayed side by side. The Holy Spirit came, just as Jesus promised. The air turned into fire and wind, and every believer was overcome by God's presence.

During that time, a feast known as pentecost was taking place in Jerusalem. People from all over the world were there. God's Spirit gave the disciples the supernatural ability to speak the languages of the other people groups, and they began sharing Jesus with everyone.

Peter led the way with a sermon from the upstairs doorway. People gathered from everywhere to hear what Peter was talking about. He taught everyone about Jesus' life, death, and resurrection. His story was so captivating that more than three thousand people became believers.

Now that the church was growing, it began to take shape. Each new believer was baptized. They came together as a group every day in the temple courts. They met in each other's homes and shared meals. They prayed with each other. They gave away their possessions and sold them to provide money for people who needed it. They sang songs and praised God together. They shared the good news of Jesus with everyone around them. They listened to the apostles teach about Jesus and obeyed everything that they learned.

And God continued to bless them and make them grow even more.

Blow Past the Roadblocks

"I don't understand those 'other' people." By design, your

church has many different kinds of people. You are young. They are old. You are one color. Someone else is another. You're a guy (or girl). She (or he) is not. You like guitar. They like piano. You prefer songs with a fast beat. They like the old hymns. Does this mean that you are doomed to disagree? Hardly. It means you are a diverse group of people that God has placed together for a purpose. He wants you to use your differences to your advantage (1 Cor. 12:12–27).

Jesus spent three years working with twelve very different people. Some of them were fishermen. Simon (not Simon Peter) was a Zealot—a rebel who wanted to kick the Romans all the way back to Rome. Peter was always opening his big mouth. Thomas was always doubting. James and John thought they were the "coolest." Judas stole funds from the moneybag. Philip was always asking questions. In spite of their differences, Jesus managed to pull them together and make them one, cohesive (really, really sticky) unit.

The same disciples, with a replacement for Judas, then followed Jesus' example and took the world by storm. They said what Jesus said. They did what Jesus did. Soon, they were the leaders of a church of considerable size. New believers came from all over the world, and all of them were very, very different. Their differences didn't slow them down; they made the church even more powerful.

If you don't understand someone else in your church, then it's time you did something about it. Volunteer to help out the senior citizens with one of their events. Offer to baby-sit in the church nursery one week. Spend a day in the summer working in your church's office. Do *something* to break out of your little shell and spend some time with those "other" people so that you can get to know them better. Then learn to celebrate your differences and work together to accomplish God's plan for your church.

"I don't know what my role is in the church." Let's see, is it pew potato? No. Maybe worship service critic? That's not it. How about chief giggle box? Negative. One more try. I know! Pastor impersonator! Nope. Now what?

You've got the Creator of the universe—Jesus—living inside you. The same Spirit who came to the disciples on the day of pentecost now burns in your soul. The Spirit of God talks to you every day about His plan for your life in the church. The burning question is, are you listening?

The Bible makes it very plain that different people in the church have different gifts (1 Cor. 12:4–7). If you don't know what these gifts are, or you are unsure of what your specific gift is, then pray about it. Ask God to show you what your gifts are. Talk to your friends about it. Go to your pastor, student pastor, and/or Bible study teacher, and ask what they think. Your spiritual gifts, combined with your talents, abilities, and interests, can be guides to help you determine where God may be leading you to serve in your church. The key is to know that God *is* calling you to serve in *some specific way* in your church. He needs you. He wants to use you.

If you read Acts 2:42–47 again, you will see that the early church met for five distinct reasons. First, they met to worship God through praise and prayer. Second, they devoted themselves to discipleship (learning how to become more like Jesus) by listening to and obeying their leaders. Third, they engaged in evangelism (sharing Jesus with other people). Fourth, they reached out to their community through ministry by selling their possessions and helping those in need. Fifth, they constantly came together in large groups and small groups for fellowship (close companionship). Overall, they became one well-oiled machine working to make Jesus the center of attention in Jerusalem.

So don't shrug your shoulders as if you don't know what your purpose in the church is. Get in there and find out. Investigate. Pray. Learn. Ask. Then when God shows you an opening for ministry in an area that really lights your fire, jump in there. Help set up for the youth group meeting. Or clean up after it's over. Maybe you can help run sound and lights or assist with computer graphics. The church Web site might need a new Web master. You could send postcards and make phone calls to people you haven't seen in church for a while. There are literally hundreds of openings in your church to serve; go find one and plug in.

"I can't possibly make a difference in this big place." It took one shy Sunday school teacher to awkwardly share Jesus with a young shoe salesman named Dwight Moody in Boston in 1858. It took one Dwight to become a traveling evangelist and rekindle the spirits of a pastor named Fred Meyer in England in 1879. It took one Fred to travel to America to preach at a college where he led a student named

Wilbur Chapman to the Lord. It took one Wilbur to hire a young Christian named Billy Sunday to work for him in leading evangelistic revivals. It took one Billy to put together a revival in North Carolina that so shook the city of Charlotte that they planned another one with a speaker named Mordecai Hamm. It took one Mordecai to preach so intensely about Jesus at that revival that a sixteen-year-old boy named Billy Graham gave his heart to Jesus. If any one of these men had said, "What can I possibly do to make a difference?" and given up, then there would be no Billy Graham today. Billy Graham has preached for more than fifty years and traveled the entire world, leading literally millions of people to know Jesus.

What difference could one man named Jesus—who lived more than two thousand years ago, ministering publicly for only three years of His life before He was executed—possibly make in the world today? What could a loud-mouthed fisherman called Peter ever do to change the course of history? What could a nameless face in the crowd like yourself ever accomplish to change the world?

You can make a difference if you let God work in you, even if it means awkwardly sharing Jesus with a friend. You might be afraid to sing in front of other people, but perhaps God wants to use your voice to share His love with others. Maybe you like to study the Bible, and God now wants you to share what you have learned with others. Do you like to write? Maybe God is calling you to be a Christian author. Perhaps you're good at math. Perhaps God will help you share Jesus with a student whom you tutor. Opportunity is knocking on a thousand doors down the corridor of your life. Open every door you come across, and see what God has in store for you. Read Ephesians 2:10 for further study.

Bum It Home

Jesus didn't just tell His disciples what to do in the church. He showed them with three years of friendship and hundreds of examples. He gave them the Spirit as a teacher. He gave them the Bible to keep them on track. The disciples, in turn, chose to do more than just talk about Jesus once a week at a church meeting. They met together every day. They shared Jesus with everyone they met. They prayed. They reached out to their community. You, too, can be a vital part of God's plan in your local church.

Here are a whole lot of ideas to try. Pick the ones that seem to interest you the most, and check with your pastor or youth pastor to see where you fit best.

➡ Get involved in the *worship* ministry of your church or youth group. Maybe you can play an instrument or sing. See if there is an opening to run lights or sound. Find out if you can help with computer slide shows or video production. Maybe you can help set up or tear down the room that everyone will use to worship. Form a prayer warrior group that meets fifteen minutes prior to worship to ask God to move in people's lives during the service.

➤ Plug into the *discipleship* ministry. Be an active part of at least one small group Bible study where you can learn more about God. Ask your teacher if you can assist in making preparations for each week. Send postcards or E-mails to people in your class, encouraging them to continue coming to class and growing in the Christian life. If you sense God's leading, see if there is an opening to actually teach a small group Bible study in your church.

⇒ Dive head over heels into the *evangelism* ministry of your church. Find out which of your friends and acquaintances do not know Jesus, and ask them to come to a weekly meeting or special event. Learn to share the entire plan of salvation with someone. Work with your church leaders to plan, set up for, and participate in events that are geared toward reaching non-Christians. If your church has regular mission trips, go on as many as you can.

➡ Plunge into the *service* ministry of your church. Work with your church to provide food to needy families at Thanksgiving or presents at Christmas. Go to a nursing home, and spend time with the residents. Help organize a canned food drive for your local food pantry. Find out what your church can do to assist your local crisis pregnancy center in helping pregnant women bring their children safely into the world.

➡ Get involved in the *fellowship* ministry. Help plan and

organize fun outings for your age group. Make sure that everyone feels included; don't let anyone feel like a reject or a nobody. See if your parents will let a group from your church come over for a party one Saturday. Become an official "greeter" at your church services so guests feel welcome.

⇝ If you have a youth pastor, do your part in helping him with the overall student ministry. Volunteer during the summer by spending at least one day or afternoon a week helping your youth pastor plan activities. You can make copies, contact other students, make calendars, or do any number of other things. Take it an extra step by encouraging your friends to volunteer as well. Keep your youth pastor staffed with volunteers all year long.

→ Your church leaders work hard to serve you. They need your encouragement and your prayers—more than you can possibly imagine. Make a commitment to pray for at least one church leader every day. Your list can include the pastor, other staff members, your student pastor, and Bible study group leaders. Remember to write encouraging notes to your leaders occasionally to tell them how much you appreciate the sacrifices they make.

Reflect

1. On a scale from one to ten, with ten being the highest, how would you rank yourself in how well you are serving

in your church? Are you satisfied with your score? What do you sense that God is calling you to do in your church family? What's stopping you? Get moving.

2. The secular world encourages you to be a rugged, self-made individual. Be your own boss. Stand on your own two feet. Rise to the top. Make your millions. Step on whoever you have to so that you can climb the corporate ladder. In contrast, God encourages members of His church to work together, like the parts of a human body. Are you trying to serve God alone, or are you working closely with other members of your church to accomplish God's plans?

3. The opening illustration of this chapter talks about a dysfunctional church that struggled with strife and division. Do you think your church is experiencing unity or division? What issues divide your church? How is your church united? What role can you play in helping the members of the church become closer?

4. The word that Jesus used for "church" means literally "the called-out ones." The idea behind this word is that the church is a group of people called out of the world by God to work together toward a common goal. What do you see as the primary role of your church or student ministry in your community? What are your church's strengths and weaknesses? What can you do to help your church fulfill its specific purpose?

5. A "mission statement" is a one-sentence description of a person's purpose in life. For example, the mission statement of the Coca-Cola Company might be "to provide tasty soft drinks for every person on the planet." Jesus' mission statement was "to seek and save the lost" (Luke 19:10). What is your mission statement? Write a one-sentence description of what you believe to be your purpose in your church. Then post that mission statement in a place where you can read it regularly to encourage you to live up to your mission.

12

PEOPLE WHO NEED ENCOURAGEMENT

Maybe I should just quit, *Mrs. Hubbard thought.* All of these years don't seem to have made much of a difference in the lives of my students. I've wasted my life, and for what? *She folded her arms in self-pity and sat down behind her scuffed old desk, debating whether or not to accept the early retirement offered to her by the school district.*

Earlier in the day, she had caught several of her students cheating on a simple vocabulary test. One class was so disruptive that she threw up her hands and walked out. The school administrators had chastised her for leaving her class unattended. She was grading papers and realized that most of her students did not read the instructions or did not care what they wrote.

Mrs. Hubbard's husband sometimes made fun of her for "wasting your life trying to teach a bunch of ruffians how to read and enjoy literature." Though her own passion for reading and writing had never dwindled, she began to think she could never inspire anyone else to appreciate the English language or the creative works that came from it.

She had taught for twenty-five years, and that was enough—at least in her mind. She thumbed through the early retirement package and decided in a single moment that she should indeed quit. Tomorrow is the last day of school, *she thought.* It will be my last day for good.

Mrs. Hubbard took the papers home and signed them, planning to take them by the administration building after school the next day. The school's final event for the day was a campuswide awards assembly where students received certificates of achievement for their excellence in academics and sports. Mrs. Hubbard sat alone in the back of the auditorium, wanting the day to end so she could go home and forget that she ever worked at the school.

Finally the principal stood up and returned to the microphone, presumably to issue closing remarks. "My fellow administrators, teachers, and students. This year we have a new award, and we want to present it in a very special way. Mrs. Hubbard, would you please come up here?"

Mrs. Hubbard sat up, unsure if she heard her name or if she imagined it. Everyone looked expectantly at her, so she made her way down the narrow row of seats, then down the aisle and to the front of the auditorium. Since I'm the oldest teacher on staff, *she reasoned,* they probably want me to present the award.

"Would you please take a seat right here, Mrs. Hubbard?"

She looked around, bewildered. One lone chair on the stage, half facing the crowd and the podium, awaited. She sat down nervously, not sure what to expect next.

A middle-aged man emerged from the back and stepped to the microphone. "Mrs. Hubbard," he began, "you may not remember me. My name is Shane Blackmon. I was in your very first class twenty-five years ago this year. When I walked into your class that first day, I hated English. I was a senior in high school and figured I knew all the English I needed to know. But nine months later when I walked out, I couldn't get enough of it. I began reading books like there was no tomorrow. I developed a love for writing, though you'd probably laugh because I never made better than a C on any of your papers. I majored in English in college. And now—and please try not to laugh—I'm an English teacher, too, and I have a Ph.D. I teach at an Ivy League school." Dr. Blackmon continued, and Mrs. Hubbard broke into tears as she began to remember her first (and very difficult) year of school when he and other students just didn't seem to care.

Dr. Blackmon finished his story and then stood behind Mrs. Hubbard. Then a woman walked to the microphone and told her story. Then another and another. Ten

---

Check It Out . . .

After Peter denied Jesus three times, he ran away and wept bitterly. He was a defeated, ashamed, and broken man, only a shadow of his former self. Jesus sensed that Peter needed encouragement, so He lovingly gave it. Just as Peter had denied Jesus three times, so Jesus gave him the chance to express his love for Jesus three times (see John 21:15–19). Jesus restored him with words of encouragement.

former students from her twenty-five-year career stood and shared how their lives were changed because of Mrs. Hubbard's English class. One by one, they embraced her and stood behind her on the stage. When the last speaker had finished, the principal returned. The auditorium erupted in applause and an unexpected standing ovation. The English teacher was in tears, not knowing how to respond.

The principal finally managed to motion everyone to silence and said, "Mrs. Hubbard, I've heard a very vicious rumor that the school district is trying to get you to retire this year." Boos and hisses erupted in protest. Continuing, he said, "I for one would like to be the first to say, 'Don't you dare.' We love you, Mrs. Hubbard. And we are proud as a student body to present you with our very first lifetime achievement award."

Mrs. Hubbard choked back the happy sobs as one of her current students brought in a beautiful crystal plaque engraved with her name, her years of service, and a quote from Mark Twain (her favorite author) that said, "Education consists mainly in what we have unlearned."

"Thank you, Mrs. Hubbard, for helping us unlearn so many things so that we could appreciate what the English language could do for our lives."

Mrs. Hubbard didn't retire. How could she? She was so inspired by seeing the fruits of her labor that she wanted to keep right on going for another twenty-five years. Her school gave her the one gift that no one else could have—encouragement. In a matter of minutes she changed her mind and decided to change the course of her life.

Jesus knows what it is like to feel discouraged. All during His life He faced hardships and suffering, and yet He constantly found the time to encourage people around Him. On one particular day, He decided to sneak up behind some men and surprise them with encouragement of His own.

Jesus' Example (Luke 24:13–48)

Cleo and James walked sullenly down the steep, winding path. The city walls of Jerusalem towered behind and above them, offering no solace for their Sunday travels. The early afternoon shadows enshrouded their cloaked figures as they began the two-hour, seven-mile walk back to Emmaus.

For the first thirty minutes, neither of them spoke. The only sound to be heard was the distant haggling in the city marketplace. That wasn't enough to penetrate the two heavy hearts that trudged onward. *How could this have happened?* they kept asking themselves.

Cleo finally broke the silence. "I can't believe this. I mean, I really thought that Jesus was the One, you know?"

James nodded sadly in agreement. "Do you remember how He came riding into Jerusalem one week ago today on that donkey? Everyone was calling Him the Messiah and laying down palm branches in His path. I was sure He was fulfilling the prophecy from Zechariah. And the way He talked! No one has ever spoken like that man before. I was ready to follow

Him until my dying breath. I never thought I would have to watch His . . . " His voice trailed off as the reality of Friday's events returned.

James tried in vain to find the right words to say, but they escaped him. Finally with nothing else to do except relive the horror, he added, "How could He go from that victory on Sunday to that tree on Friday? Are we just stupid to have believed this wandering Teacher? Where did we go wrong? How did we get so caught up in Him? We must be blind!"

He was more angry than he was depressed. James said, "Do you see how stupid we are? We've been fooled! The true Messiah, when He comes, will conquer the Romans and kick those Pharisees in the behind, not die helplessly on a tree. The Bible says that anyone who hangs on a tree is cursed. Jesus is cursed—and so are we for believing."

Cleo wanted to argue with his friend's logic, but he didn't know how. Jesus was dead. He bled to death in front of their eyes on a cross—the most shameful way a man could die. They kept thinking He would come down. They kept thinking a miracle would happen. They were wrong.

As the late afternoon sun beat down on them, they continued to talk about what they had seen when another traveler going in the same direction came up behind them. "Good day, my friends. Isn't it an incredible day? So, what's going on? What are you two guys talking about? May I join in the conversation?"

Cleo was amazed that someone could be happy at a time like this. "Um, hello," he began. "You've obviously just come from Jerusalem. Didn't you see or hear what happened this weekend?"

"I have no idea what you are talking about. Let me in on it. What happened?"

It pained Cleo to have to tell the story all over again and relive the memories. "A man named Jesus from the city of Nazareth was here. He was a mighty prophet of God. His words were to the heart like fire is to dry wood. He performed miracles. He healed people. He spoke the truth. We were certain that He was the Messiah. And yet . . . "

Cleo cleared his throat and clenched his fists, trying hard not to let his anger show. He said, "The Pharisees and chief priests were jealous. They were losing their power and influence over the crowds. So, out of envy, they kidnapped Him, arrested Him, and made up lies about laws that He had broken. They stirred up the crowds to pressure Pilate into giving him the death penalty. All this happened in a matter of hours! Finally Jesus was sentenced to be crucified in the place of Barabbas, a murderer. They beat Him. They forced Him to carry His cross to Golgotha. They nailed Him to a tree and laughed as He hung there in pain and shame. Finally by midafternoon Friday, He died. We saw this with our own eyes.

"Then early this morning as we were preparing to leave, some women came running back from the garden tomb and claimed that His body was no longer there. They said angels had appeared to them and told them that Jesus was alive. People, including those women, are so upset by these events that they are hallucinating."

The traveler listened without interruption until this point. As Cleo finished his story and kicked the ground in despair, the stranger spoke. "So you think that because of what you saw, Jesus cannot be the Messiah? Why do you give up so soon? The events you just described to me sound exactly like what the Bible has said must happen to the Messiah."

As they walked, the traveler started with the book of Genesis and went all the way through Malachi, quoting Scriptures and explaining how each one revealed that the Messiah must suffer, die, and rise from the dead in order to save His people from their sin.

The traveler talked until they reached Emmaus and acted as if he would then continue on his journey. Cleo and James begged him to come inside for dinner. "It's too late to travel. Join us!" James said.

The stranger agreed and came inside. James prepared a simple meal of bread, fruit, and fish. They sat down at the table and asked the traveler if he would offer thanks. Their new friend said a heartfelt prayer and, as was the custom, picked up a piece of bread and broke it into pieces. As he reached across the table to hand the bread to Cleo and James, both of them suddenly recognized the face of the stranger who sat across from them. It was Jesus! Cleo jumped to his feet in amazement, only to see that Jesus was no longer there. He had disappeared!

James said, "We've got to go back to Jerusalem! Those women weren't hallucinating. They were telling the truth! I felt as if my heart was on fire while He was talking to us on the way home. He knew what He was talking about because He *is* the Messiah. Come on!"

Back the two ran to Jerusalem as fast as they could. Several times they stopped from sheer exhaustion, but soon pressed on. An hour later, they arrived at the city and found Jesus' disciples huddled together in an upstairs room where they had shared their last meal with Jesus.

The Eleven were talking excitedly, each sharing stories that Jesus had been seen. Simon Peter was all smiles and said, "He came to me this morning as I walked alone in my despair. He is alive!" Cleo and James shared their story as well, and everyone was amazed. They were asking questions to learn more when, unexpectedly, the dimly lit room grew immediately bright—as if light were coming from every direction. There, standing in the middle of the group, was Jesus. He said one word to them, "Peace."

They froze. *It's a ghost!* they thought. No one moved or said a word. Jesus realized their fears and said, "Hey, it's Me! Don't be scared. Don't doubt. I'm no ghost. Does a ghost have flesh and bones like Me? Touch Me! Pinch Me! Look at the nail holes in My hands and feet. It's Me. I'm here."

Still no one moved. Some believed. Some did not. Jesus said, "Okay, I'll prove it to you. Have you ever seen a ghost actually eat food?" With that, He asked for some fish and proceeded to eat it in front of them. "There. Now do you believe Me?"

As if by magic, suddenly their hearts were opened, and they began to understand. Jesus explained from the Bible why everything that had happened was all part of God's plan.

It all fit. It all made sense. "You are My witnesses," Jesus said. "You've seen all of this with your own eyes. Now it is your turn to go out and explain it to others so that their heavy hearts can hear this good news as well."

Blow Past the Roadblocks

"I'm not even sure what the problem is." You see someone who is discouraged. He's depressed. He hurts inside. You have no idea what is going on, so do you shrug your shoulders and walk away? Of course not! You ask what the problem is. You sit down and talk. You *listen*.

Jesus knows the importance of letting a discouraged person talk it out. He knew exactly what was wrong, but He still asked. He let those two men air out their feelings and share their problem. He didn't interrupt. He didn't condemn. He *listened*.

Learn to ask and listen when someone needs encouragement. Don't try to solve everything right away—just listen. Sometimes it may take hours or even days for the real heart of the matter to come out in the open. Don't interrupt, and don't condemn. Learn the entire problem before you offer a response.

"I don't have time." Listening takes time. Healing takes time. If you're going to help someone get out of the dumps, you'll have to give up time.

On the first day that Jesus rose from the dead, can you imagine what kind of schedule He must have had? "Let's see. First I've got to kick Satan's tail end—I've been wanting to do *that* for the last thirty-three years. Then I need to see the women at my tomb. Then on to Simon Peter and the other disciples. My mom needs to see Me alive and then . . . " Jesus had a full plate. And yet He took a few *hours* out of the day to sneak up on a couple of discouraged travelers and offer them compassionate encouragement. He even joined them for dinner. He didn't need to eat—He's God! But He sat down with them anyway to help make them smile.

When you're down, which would you rather have: someone who looks you in the eye, or someone who checks her watch and says, "I really need to be going now"? You want someone who's willing to give up her regularly scheduled programming to focus on you. That's the kind of person you need to be when you're encouraging someone else. Sit down. Hear him out. Look him in the eye. Relax. Sacrifice your other plans. Stay with him for a while.

Fan the Flame!

"He heals the brokenhearted and binds up their wounds" (Psalm 147:3 NIV). A word of encouragement can do wonders for a discouraged heart. All around you, dejected people need words of affirmation, encouragement, and compassion. Be God's voice and extend His encouragement to them.

"I don't have the answers." If you are walking home one evening and notice a neighbor's house engulfed in flames, would you walk away because you aren't trained in fighting

fires? No way! You'd grab the nearest phone and dial 911. You would get someone who does have the answers right away.

The same holds true for helping someone in a bind. If she is discouraged about a problem you know nothing about, you simply call Someone who does know—Jesus.

Jesus used the Word of God, the Bible, to encourage His downtrodden companions. He applied different passages of Scripture to the situation at hand, and it made those men's hearts catch fire. Their depression began to subside. Their eyes started to open. Their love for life returned. In the middle of all of their struggles, they finally realized that Jesus was right there all along.

Most people get depressed because they see no hope—no light at the end of the tunnel. They feel that they have been abandoned and that nothing will change their situation. That's where you come in. You can do two things. First, pray. Go to Jesus, and ask Him to help you encourage your friend. Second, be familiar with the Bible and how it applies to your friend's situation. Read him Romans 8:28, Jeremiah 29:11–13, or any other passage that God puts on your heart. Talk about a person in the Bible who was in a similar situation and managed to get through it. Nothing soothes a wounded soul more than the Word of God applied with love at the right time and place.

Burn It Home

Jesus did more than listen. He did more than give His time. He did more than use God's Word as an ointment. He considered each person's individual despair and touched him accordingly. There's a small verse in this story that you may have overlooked. Luke 24:34 says that Jesus had risen and appeared to Simon (Peter). Do you remember Peter's recent track record? He cut off a man's ear, and Jesus told him to put the sword away. He ran away as Jesus was being arrested. Three times during the night he denied that he even knew Jesus. The Bible says that after Peter's denial, he wept bitterly. Peter was discouraged, perhaps more than anyone else. To remedy that, Jesus decided that a one-on-one encounter was necessary. He appeared to Peter before He appeared to any of the other disciples, just so He could encourage him.

Go the distance. Burn it home. Show your compassion by encouraging the people around you who are down.

➤ Sometimes the written word can be very powerful to someone who is down in the dumps. If you know someone who needs a pick-me-up, find the perfect card, and write a note of encouragement inside. Send an E-mail. Write a letter. Include a Bible verse. The recipient can read the words again and again, applying them like medicine for the heart.

➤ Widows and orphans are two distinct groups of people that often need extra encouragement. The loss of a spouse or absence of parents can be devastating. James 1:27 specifically mentions these two groups as sensitive to distress. You can help them in their loneliness. Visit a nursing home, orphanage, or the home of a widow in your neighborhood on a regular basis. Volunteer once a week or month to drop by just for a visit. Adopt one particular person as your "grandmother" or "brother/sister" and spend extra time with him or her.

➥ The death of a friend, a family member, or even a longtime pet can bring anyone down. When someone you know loses a loved one, make time to be there. Go to the funeral. Send flowers. Take food to the house so that no one has to worry about making dinner. If you know the person who died, talk about any good memories you have. If the deceased was a Christian, remind everyone that you will see him again in heaven.

⇒ Thanksgiving and Christmas seasons are supposed to be happy times, but many people without families and friends find the last two months of the year to be the most discouraging of all. Spread the joy God has blessed you with by inviting others to be a part of your family's celebrations. Invite a friend over for Thanksgiving if she has no other place to go. Adopt a needy child for Christmas, and provide gifts and clothes. Go Christmas caroling in your neighborhood.

→ Single parents are prone to discouragement simply because they have so much work to do on their own. Working at a job, parenting, doing housework, paying bills, and taking care of other tasks can literally drown the life out of a single mother or father. If you have only one parent in your house, be extra sensitive to the time and effort Mom or Dad gives to provide and care for you. If any of your friends have single parents, offer to baby-sit for free or help do some neglected chores.

↪ Failure is a big source of despair. You flunk the test, lose the race, get dumped by your girl. You feel as if the whole world is saying, "You don't cut it, so go dig a hole and crawl in." Everyone feels this way when he fails. Keep your eyes and ears open for signs that someone else may be discouraged because of a failure. If a buddy doesn't pass the test, help him study. If your friend loses the race, slap her on the back, and tell her she can do better next time. If your roommate loses his girlfriend, spend time with him and be available for him. Your encouragement will help get him back on his feet.

➤ Many people in the world have never seen or at least never owned a Bible. The Book of Encouragement is not in their hands. Do your part in buying extra copies of the Bible and getting them into the hands of people who need them. If you know someone who doesn't have a Bible, give him one. Many organizations collect donations to provide Bibles to people in other countries. Buy one Bible for someone else in another country who doesn't have one. The message of encouragement that you send through this gift will never be fully known until you see the results in heaven.

Reflect

1. Suicide—it's the ultimate form of discouragement. Thousands of people kill themselves every year because they know no other way out of their despair. Many times the person who commits suicide showed no outward signs of discouragement, but inside he was crying out for someone to show him the way. You can do your part in saving these lives by being an encouragement to everyone whom God has placed in your path. Wouldn't it be great to get to heaven and find out that dozens of people that you knew never considered suicide as an option because of the influence you had in their lives?

2. Write down a list of things that encourage you. Your list might include watching a good movie, hanging out with a best friend, getting gifts on your birthday, listening to your favorite comedian, or just sitting outside under the stars. Why do you think each of these things touches you in a positive way? Now, think of one person in your life who could use encouragement. Make a list of the things that would probably encourage her. Do your part in providing those special moments or things for this person.

3. Have you ever thought about the word *encourage*? The prefix *en-* means "to put into." If you have courage, then you possess a brave and confident spirit. So, Einstein, put the two together, and what do you get? *Encourage* means "to put a brave and confident spirit into" someone else.

In contrast, the prefix *dis-* means "to deprive of." If you discourage someone, then you deprive her of a brave and confident spirit. Now that the vocabulary test is over, think about the people you know. Would they say that you have a habit of *encouraging* or *discouraging* other people? Make it your goal to constantly put courage *into* the people God places in your path.

4. Read Acts 4:36; 11:22–24. These verses talk about a man named Joseph. The disciples nicknamed him Barnabas, which means "Son of Encouragement." Why do you think they nicknamed him that? What was so different about Barnabas that made him so encouraging? How much different would your life have to be for your friends to give you a nickname like this?

5. Laughter is often called the best medicine. There's some truth to that. God invented laughter, and studies show that it can actually improve health. It certainly can be a great antidote for discouragement. What can you do to spread a little more laughter and a little less gloom and doom?

6. Prayer is a powerful tool to encourage others. What you cannot do, God can. Make a prayer list of people you know who need encouragement. In addition to everything else that you do, ask God to give each person a brave and confident spirit. Don't forget to thank the Lord when He answers your prayer.

13

PEOPLE WHO ARE DIFFERENT

"Why did this have to happen to me?" Chris asked himself, looking painfully into the bathroom mirror. His face was a zit farm. The pimples were everywhere—on the end of his nose, all over his forehead, on his neck. They covered his cheeks and temples and even found their way into his eyebrows.

As if the looks weren't bad enough, the pain added injury to insult. Every time his heart beat, his blood pumped pressure into every blemish, refusing to allow him to forget that they were there. Chris turned out the light and walked away from the mirror. I hate *the way I look, Chris thought as he slammed the bathroom door shut.* I know people think I'm ugly. They can't even look me in the eye when they talk to me because my zits are getting all the attention. *Reluctantly he grabbed his backpack and headed out the door for school.*

On the bus, Chris sat alone and stared out the window. He tried to think of something other than his face and was almost successful when a voice brought him back to reality. "Hey, Pizza Face. Are you selling slices today?"

Chris looked at the source of the taunt—a junior higher two years younger than himself. Wounded deeply, he tried to fight back. "That's right. You want a piece of me? I deliver." Chris rose from his seat, knowing he had no intentions of fighting. The bluff worked. His attacker backed down and turned away. Chris slumped back into his seat and did his best not to cry.

When he arrived home later that evening, he walked through the living room past his mother and father. "Hey, Chris," his mom said. "Your face seems to be getting worse. I think we need to see a dermatologist."

Thanks, Mom! *Chris thought.* Worse! How could it possibly be worse? Everyone thinks I'm a freak. *Chris went to his room without a word and threw himself on the bed. He flipped on his TV and tried to do his homework to drown out his desperation. He couldn't concentrate. He rolled over on his back and lay there, staring at the ceiling. He cried. He prayed. He ran his fingers over the bumps on his face and cursed.*

Suddenly his phone rang. Chris sat up and cleared his throat, wondering who might be calling. He picked up the receiver. "Hello?"

"Chris," a pretty voice on the other end said. "Hi, this is Sherry. What are you doing?"

Chris's heart raced. Sherry was his crush. She was beautiful. She sat next to him in biology, and he always got nervous around her. Why would she be calling him?

"I'm just sitting here, working on geometry," he said while his voice quivered. "What are you up to?"

"Oh, nothing. I'm just bored. Listen, I started thinking about

how much fun we have in biology, you know? I mean, you really know how to make me laugh. Um, anyway, I guess what I'm trying to say is, if you don't already have plans, would you mind taking me to the homecoming dance next weekend?"

It was all he could do to keep from screaming. Me? he screamed inside. Why me? Calming himself as best he could, he said, "Sherry, do you really want to go with me? You don't already have another date? Why would you want to go with me?"

Sherry was silent for a moment and then asked, "Why wouldn't I want to go with you? I like you."

Chris nearly burst into tears. "Sherry, you've seen me. You've seen my face. Why would you want to be seen in public with me?"

"Chris," Sherry said softly, "I don't care about

> ## Check It Out . . .
>
> The perfect word has incredible potential. Read Proverbs 25:11 for a description of the value of encouragement.

that. That will go away; it's just temporary. I like what I see in you on the inside. You're nice. Sweet. Funny. Caring. Most guys aren't like that. You're different."

In a moment all of his shame melted away like ice cream on a hot summer sidewalk. "Sherry, I'd be honored to take you to homecoming. You got it."

With a single phone call, Chris's thoughts went from total despair to sheer ecstasy—all because of the kind words from someone else. Chris's situation didn't change; he still had acne. But now he had Sherry on his side, and that made all the difference in the world. Kind words to someone who is different can melt away fear and shame. Jesus once offered a few kind words to a man who really needed to hear them.

Jesus' Example (Luke 19:1–9)

Zacchaeus was a wee little man. He was so short that sometimes he had to stand on his toes just to reach the counters at the store. Everyone he knew was taller than he was. It was embarrassing. As if that weren't enough, Zacchaeus was a wealthy tax collector. Even though he was a Jew, he collected taxes for the Roman government. Many of his Jewish friends considered him a traitor, not a true Jew. To top it off, he wore an amulet around his neck to signify his position as tax collector. He was recognized wherever he went.

In his mind, Zacchaeus just knew that people were whispering about him behind his back. *They're making fun of my height,* he mused. *They hate me for collecting taxes even though it's the only job I know. I hate my life. I wish I could grow taller and change careers. Then maybe people would like me.*

Zacchaeus kicked the dirt under his feet as he walked the streets of his hometown, Jericho, on his way to work that morning. He was still feeling sorry for himself when he heard a commotion. He looked up to see a very large crowd coming his way. Wondering what was going on, he asked a traveler passing by.

"That Jesus character is in town, Short Stuff," came the stinging reply. "What's it to you?"

Jesus! Zacchaeus thought. *That's the man some say is the Son of God. Oh, I'd like to catch a glimpse of Him.* Then he sighed, looking at the crowd coming his way. *I'm so short, I won't be able to see a thing with all those people.* Analyzing the situation, Zacchaeus looked back down the way he had come and noticed several sycamore-fig trees along the side of the road. *That's it,* he thought. *That will get me the best seat in the house.*

He turned around and made his way quickly back down the road. Arriving at one of the trees, he checked to see if anyone was watching him. Then he grabbed onto the lower branches and pulled himself into the tree. He climbed up to a large overhanging limb that concealed him behind the thick leaves—hoping no one would see the poor man who was so short he had to climb a tree just to see.

As the crowd made its way closer, Zacchaeus's heart began to race. All he wanted to do was see the famous Teacher. Then he could go home and crawl back into his shell and feel sorry for himself again.

Soon the commotion arrived and began passing directly beneath Zacchaeus. He heard people shouting and begging. Everyone wanted Jesus' attention. Zacchaeus strained his eyes until finally he saw the man at the center of the crowd. *That must be Jesus,* he thought. *There's something about the look in His eyes . . .*

Suddenly, just as Jesus reached the point in the road next

to Zacchaeus's hiding place, He stopped. Zacchaeus froze, afraid that he had been spotted. Jesus looked up into the tree and pointed. *Oh, no!* Zacchaeus thought. *He's going to make me look like even more of a fool than I already am!*

"Zacchaeus," Jesus said, still pointing. "Get out of that tree right this instant. After all, if I'm going to your house for dinner, I need you to show Me how to get there."

The crowd fell silent. They looked up into the tree. There sat Zacchaeus, the man that they all hated and had made fun of so many times. "Jesus called him by name. Jesus is going to his house for *dinner*. What's up with that? Zacchaeus is bad news."

Zacchaeus didn't know what to think, but he knew that he was tired of hiding. He scrambled down from the tree and stood next to Jesus, honored to hear that Jesus wanted to come to his house. He immediately led Jesus and His disciples down the road toward his house—in front of the entire crowd.

On the way to his house, Zacchaeus felt like the tallest man in town. Jesus, the Son of God, wanted to come to *his* house. *I'm going to throw one heck of a party,* he thought. And that's just what he did. Because he was a wealthy man, Zacchaeus spared no expense. He invited everyone who could fit in the house to stay for dinner.

During the dinner, Jesus spoke about God's love for everyone—both great and small. Zacchaeus was so overwhelmed that he immediately chose to become a follower of Jesus. He jumped up from his place at the table and said, "Lord, I want to give half of everything I own to the poor.

And if I've cheated anyone in my dealings as a tax collector, I'm going to repay what I stole—four times as much."

"Do you see this man?" Jesus said in front of all the guests. "Today he has become a true child of Abraham, a true Jew." In saying this, Jesus reversed people's thinking and made Zacchaeus one of the "tallest" men in town.

Blow Past the Roadblocks

"She's just weird." You know the type. You're walking through the hallway at school, and "it" walks by—that strange entity whose mere purpose for existing eludes you. You don't get the hair, the makeup, or the clothes. You can't even look her in the eye without shuddering. You know the funny thing? She probably has the same problem with you!

Zacchaeus was weird to some people. He was really short. He was rich. He wore an amulet around his neck that identified him as a tax collector. Face it. He was the chief freakazoid. As Jesus was walking down the road, Zacchaeus was hiding in a tree. How weird is that? Jesus could have pretended not to see him and just walked on by. Instead, He invited Himself over to dinner.

Don't let outward appearances keep you from touching someone else's life with a little compassion. Invite "it" to your church. Pray for her. Get to know the weirdo who sits next to you in class. Find out more about the group that sits at the "other" table in the cafeteria.

"What would everybody else think?" You've got to protect

your rep, so you can't be seen talking to the local freak. Imagine that the new kid in school is really bizarre, and everyone else starts laughing behind his back and talking about him. Are you going to stand up for him or just laugh right along? What if you have a chance to meet him? Will you be extra friendly or move to the other side of the room?

Jesus had people following Him for miles around. There were pretty women and powerful men in His entourage. He definitely had a rep going. So why would He stop in the middle of the road—in front of everyone—and pretend to be friends with the likes of Zacchaeus? Because He knew that Zacchaeus needed the most attention right then. He didn't care what people thought. He did what He knew was best.

Who cares what people think? Sure, you want to be accepted, but so does that person everyone is making fun of. Who is going to accept *him*? God may be calling you to be the first. Others will follow.

Fan the Flame!

Jesus never avoided the freaks. In fact, He was a friend to the "worst" of sinners—the tax collectors, prostitutes, and lepers. He was willing to touch the untouchable. His love transcended all else.

"*He's evil.*" This is not a bad excuse. If someone you know is different in a bad sort of way, perhaps it's not the best idea for you to be hanging out with him. However, are you sure that you're right about this guy, or is it just prejudice?

Lots of people in Jericho thought of Zacchaeus as an evil man. They assumed all tax collectors were national traitors and crooks and that abnormally short people were cursed by God. Those assumptions ran deep, and it was a huge shock to see Jesus chumming up with Zacchaeus and going to his house. Jesus didn't care whether the assumptions were true or not. He knew that Zacchaeus needed God, and so He delivered.

Play it safe—sure. Don't do something stupid that would endanger your life. But remember, those "evil" people of the world are the ones who need Jesus the most. If God prompts you to reach out to someone like that, don't be afraid to follow His leading. And remember, the person may not be as evil as you think. Maybe he just wears that face to scare everyone away. Come back at him with the face of Jesus, and let him know that God loves him.

Bum It Home

Jesus did more than just say hello to Zacchaeus. He did more than shake his hand and call him by name. He did more than go to his house for a party. He made sure the whole town knew He was doing all of these things. It was an in-your-face way of saying, "This guy is with Me. He's cool. He's all right. And I, for one, am not ashamed to be hanging out with him."

That's how Jesus wants you to make people who are "different" feel too.

➡ People with mental disabilities are often thought of as different. People with Down's syndrome, autism, Alzheimer's, or similar problems often get labeled as crazy or stupid. They are nothing of the kind. Their brains just don't compute their surroundings in the same way that yours does. So be kind. If you notice someone working at a grocery store or walking down the street who seems a little "off" to you, go out of your way to smile and say hello. If you see a parent pushing a baby girl with Down's syndrome, lean down and comment how beautiful she is. Remember, they are God's children too.

⇨ Older people can sometimes be so different that you just don't want to have anything to do with them. The way they dress, the way they drive, the way they talk, the traditions they have—all are very different from yours. Don't let that make you thumb your nose. You need those people. One day you will *be* those people. Respect them. Hold the door open for them. Ask for their advice. Help them with the heavy stuff. Treat them as you would your own grandparents.

⇨ Have you ever noticed that even in our modern society, we still have trouble getting along with people who have a different skin color from our own? Whites, blacks,

Hispanics, Asians, Native Americans—our country is a beautiful melting pot of all of these and more. Go out of your way to treat people of different nationalities kindly. Show them that you have no prejudice or ill will. If you find yourself the victim of racism, refuse to fight back. Turn the other cheek. Show compassion in return.

→ Money can play a role in making you different from someone else. If you are middle class, then the rich and the poor are foreign to you. You probably envy the rich and pity the poor. If you find yourself in one of the two extremes, maybe you really have a hard time identifying with your opposite. Regardless of where you stand on the money scale, you should never let dollar signs keep you from showing compassion to others. Do your best to help the poor. Volunteer to serve at a soup kitchen or homeless shelter. Give money to organizations that minister to the poor.

⇒ Are you smart in school, or do you struggle just to pass? Intelligence makes us different. Not everyone is smart, and there's no shame in being gifted in areas besides brain power. If you're a bookworm, treat your intellectually challenged peers with humility and friendliness. If you're not a brain, don't make fun of those who are.

Reflect

1. Have you ever treated someone unkindly simply because

he was different from you? Make a list of people or groups to whom you need to show more compassion in spite of your differences.

2. Hate crimes are a growing trend in our culture. People become victims of a crime simply because they are different. Name the types of people you know who have been attacked for being different. In each case, who is persecuting whom? Why? What would you do to stop hate crimes if you were president of the United States? What would you do to stop hate crimes if you were a child of the Creator? You may not be president, but you are a child of God—and that's enough to make a world of difference.

3. In the Old Testament, Genesis 30–50 tells the story of a man named Joseph. He was different. He was so different that his brothers hated him. They sold him as a slave, pocketed the money, and told their father that he had died. Joseph was a stranger in a strange country for many years, until one day he had a chance to get back at his brothers. Read his story, and learn the right and wrong ways to treat people in your life who are different.

CHECK IT OUT!
GET INVOLVED!
MAKE A DIFFERENCE!

Compassion International
God can use you to change the life of a child forever.
www.ci.org

Habitat for Humanity International
A Christian organization that welcomes volunteers from all faiths who are committed to Habitat's goal of eliminating poverty housing.
www.habitat.org

World Vision
For kids in need around the world, hope changes everything.
www.worldvision.org

National Center for Family Literacy
Promoting family literacy services across the United States.
www.famlit.org

Big Brothers, Big Sisters of America
Making a big difference. One child at a time.
www.bbbsa.org

Americares
Bringing help and hope.
www.americares.org

Volunteermatch.org
Thousands of volunteer opportunities on-line.
www.volunteermatch.org